PREDICTION AND FULFILLMENT
IN THE BIBLE

PREDICTION
AND FULFILLMENT
IN THE BIBLE

by
Gurdon C. Oxtoby

The Westminster Press
Philadelphia

LIBRARY OF CONGRESS CATALOG CARD NO. 66–20094

PUBLISHED BY THE WESTMINSTER PRESS®
PHILADELPHIA, PENNSYLVANIA

PRINTED IN THE UNITED STATES OF AMERICA

To my family

Contents

I. The Problem   9

II. The Uses of Scripture   19

III. The Accumulation of Hebrew Scripture   46

IV. Prophecy and Prediction   62

V. The Categories of Fulfillment   94
    The Kingly Messiah   96
    The Son of Man   102
    The Ideal Prophet   106
    Perfect Priest and Perfect Sacrifice   109
    The Servant of the Lord   113
    The New Covenant   117
    Summary   118

VI. The Biblical Faith of the Church   122

Subject Index   151

Index of Scripture References   155

CHAPTER I

The Problem

LARGE NUMBERS of people today consider the Bible to be irrelevant. This is the latter half of the twentieth century, and the Bible was written long ago. New discoveries in the world about us are of almost daily occurrence. Unprecedented problems urgently clamor to be answered. New technological processes are changing our way of life. Our civilization seems far removed from that of Biblical times. In the atomic age a growing suspicion arises that a book written so long ago has little to say to our time. A feeling prevails with many that the Bible belongs to an age that has passed away. True, it may be a literary product of the past, perhaps significant to those who are historically-minded. But does it have more than passing interest for modern men whose concerns are in the present century?

A variety of reasons contribute to this prevalent attitude toward the Bible. In the first place, *the Bible is not always easy to read*. This is less true now than before the appearance of translations into modern English; but when the Bible was available almost exclusively in the seventeenth-century language of the King James Version, its very style seemed to support the impression that the book belonged to the past. It was not infrequently referred to as a "monument of English literature," a statement that did little to dispel the impression of antiquity. Even with the appearance of translations into contemporary English, the former attitude that the Bible is out-of-date prevails in many circles.

In the second place, for many people *the Bible is hard to understand*. The words may be intelligible, but the ideas are not. They reflect the times in which it was composed. Its social and political background is that of the Middle East over a period of more than twelve hundred years, from the early beginnings of the Hebrew people to the first century of the Christian era. In order to comprehend the numerous references to ancient Israel and such neighboring nations as Egypt, Assyria, Babylonia, Greece, and Rome, the reader must have some knowledge of the ancient world. Not everyone does. If he does not know the situations faced by the Old Testament prophets, he has difficulty understanding what they had to say. Unless he knows something of the conditions faced by Christians in New Testament times, the issues that concern the writers of the New Testament books are sometimes less than clear. To understand the significance of what is set down, a modern reader must bring to the study of the Bible a knowledge that many do not have. Lack of comprehension accounts for much widespread suspicion that it is irrelevant to our day.

A third hazard is that sometimes *the Bible is hard to believe*. Not only does it contain accounts of happenings that are seemingly incredible to the modern mind, but the view of the world reflected there is different from our view. It proceeds from assumptions that are at variance with those on which we in the culture of our time base decisions and actions. We cannot believe, as the Biblical world seems to, that we live on a flat earth beneath which there is an underworld called Sheol and above which is a heaven, unless these are figures of speech. Can we really believe that Moses, climbing Mt. Sinai, could receive ten commandments, " written with the finger of God " (Ex. 31:18; Deut. 9:10)?

It may be noted that one of the plagues experienced by the Egyptians just before the exodus of Israel is also termed " the finger of God " (Ex. 8:19), which suggests that this phrase is symbolic. To what extent are other descriptions also symbolic? Would this symbolic aspect make the Bible easier to believe?

Still another difficulty is that for many persons *the Bible is hard to affirm as authoritative*. In an atmosphere in which every basic concept of life is open to scrutiny and reevaluation, it is proper to reexamine our view of the Bible. Positions long cherished should be looked at once again to determine their validity. Here we discover that the kind of authority ascribed to the Bible in other centuries no longer appears reasonable. We cannot affirm with the easy assurance of former generations that here is an infallible book, whose statements are binding on men today, inerrant in all its parts, to be accepted or rejected as a whole. A great many impossible views about the Bible have been insisted on. Not infrequently voices are heard advocating a return to some view that prevailed in the past. The erroneous supposition that we must profess to believe something about the Bible that we cannot in good conscience affirm is uncalled for. Nevertheless, it is a hazard to many in preventing full understanding of what the Bible is.

By many, then, the Bible has been shelved, or, at best, tabled. It remains a closed book. Though we hear it read in church, we feel that it has ambiguities about it that are not resolved. We wish we might include it more definitely in our religious experience, and we are aware of the regard in which it has long been held, but we wish to be honest with ourselves. It will not do to put our religious faith into a different category from that with which we regard other aspects of human knowledge. It is incumbent upon us to search for a view of Scripture that is both satisfying and consistent with the facts as we observe them. Such a view will be proposed in these pages.

Is Scripture Fulfilled?

Modern literary and historical approaches to the Bible have removed some of the mystical and dogmatic attitudes that prevailed in other generations. We now regard the various books contained there as arising out of definite historical settings. Linguistic studies enable scholars to determine with more probability what the words actually meant. But we also ask why these words were spoken or written, to whom they were addressed, and what were the conditions they were intended to meet. We also inquire what sources may have been used, and whether additions or alterations may have been made to the original statements. On the basis of such factual information we are then in a better position to estimate the significance or value of the book, in its original use, and in subsequent times.

Nowhere, perhaps, is the problem of the contemporary interpreter more perplexing than in the whole matter of prediction and fulfillment. Many of the writers of the New Testament books assert that a certain course of events occurred, fulfilling words that had been spoken or written many centuries earlier. Not only are New Testament events seen as happening according to ancient words, but it is implied that the seers of centuries long past foresaw the New Testament developments. This kind of thing seems to the modern mind to border on the incredible. It seems not to correspond to the way in which we customarily regard occurrences in our time.

Through the years there have been great numbers of predictions as to what shape the future would assume, but experience in the everyday world makes it clear that some of these have come to pass and others have not. Contemporary speakers and writers are prone to make statements about the days that lie ahead of us, and we accept these at their face value, knowing full well that only time will tell whether they have guessed rightly or not. But this is not quite the way in which we have been accustomed to think of the Bible. Through the years there has grown up an attitude, based on a conception of Scripture as a magical book, that regards the forecasts of the prophets in a very special light. These men are considered as having been endowed with some kind of unique and uncanny ability to see the distant future. The critical mind of today is ill-disciplined if it does not raise the question, Is prediction possible?

Let us make this position clear: Is it credible that a man living in the seventh or sixth century before Christ could, with any accuracy, predict what would not occur until hundreds of years had passed? If his world was one in which Assyria or Babylonia was the leading world power, could he foresee conditions that would prevail when Greece or Rome had succeeded them? To many honest inquirers, there is something of the magical or superstitious in such assumptions. No doubt there are considerable numbers who profess to believe that this power of prediction could be. Nevertheless, it seems to others that to do so would mean a loss of integrity. A detailed representation of the future, often claimed to be set forth in passages of Scripture, by which events of the first or the twentieth century and succeeding centuries are said to be minutely forecast by an ancient seer, seems to many of us to put the Bible into a difficult, not to say a questionable, position. It seems to obligate the reader of the Bible to attitudes and presuppositions that he rejects in all other areas of his experience. No wonder there is a widespread feeling that religion is superstition, that faith is unreasonable, and that the Old Testament prophets really belong to the age of the enchanters and sorcerers of Babylon, or the priestesses of the famous oracles of ancient Greece.

In the usage of the New Testament, one comes repeatedly upon such statements as, " Now this came to pass that the word spoken by the prophet might be fulfilled." More than twenty-five times in the Gospels alone, this or a similar phrase occurs. Numerous additional references call attention to Old Testament statements that are said to have new significance because of some Gospel event. The preachers in the book of The Acts repeatedly make reference to passages from the Old Testament, claiming significance for the work of Christ in the light of some Biblical quotation. The epistles appeal again and again to Old Testament passages to authenticate or support their doctrine.

The quotations are from all parts of the Old Testament. Not only are words of the prophets cited but passages from The Psalms, and from the books of the Pentateuch as well. Thus it is recorded that the unknown traveler on the road to Emmaus, in response to the disappointed hopes of his companions, " beginning with Moses and all the prophets . . . interpreted to them in all the scriptures the things concerning himself " (Luke 24:27). It is therefore apparent that the problem is not simply one of prediction and fulfillment of what certain Old Testament figures known as prophets had said, but a more general position, that in many places throughout the Old Testament there are foreshadowings of the New.

MODERN CLAIMS OF " PROPHETIC " GROUPS

Through centuries of Christian development, a variety of groups have arisen proclaiming that events taking place in their own day were likewise foreseen by men of old. Sects and movements within evangelical churches even today take such positions. Repeatedly we are told that we are living in " the last days," described in detail in Biblical prophecy. Appeal is made to events and personages in our time as coinciding with descriptions that are adduced from Scripture. Adventists point to the " signs of the times," and Millenarians project, on the basis of " wars and rumors of wars," the coming " tribulation," which will finally authenticate the remainder of their doctrine of the end of the age. Some are convinced. Others are incredulous. What is the sincere Christian inquirer to do? And, if he cannot accept this sort of prediction, is he in any position to take Christianity seriously at all?

An extreme example of this kind of interpretation came to my attention some years ago. A well-known minister sent me a copy of an article in a " prophetic " journal, which claimed that the eighteenth chapter of Isaiah really described the United States of America. The quotation of Hebrew phrases was included to lend authority to the position, and the minister asked for my evaluation of the claims. It seems to me that the chief allegations could be itemized as follows:

ISAIAH, CHAPTER 18

"Land of whirring wings" — a general statement that the United States is foremost in the world in aviation progress.

"Beyond the rivers of Ethiopia" — the Hebrew for "beyond" is said to mean "west of," and the first major country west of the rivers of Ethiopia is the United States.

"Which sends ambassadors by the sea" — since the United States is isolated by seas from all other countries of the world except two, ambassadors cannot go by land.

"In vessels of papyrus" — the Hebrew word for papyrus is said to be from a root that means "to drink"; therefore what is meant is "water-drinking vessels," i.e., steamships, for which the prophet had no other word.

"A nation tall and smooth" — Americans are generally taller than most other peoples, and usually are clean-shaven.

"A nation feared near and far" — obviously the United States, because of its resources and might.

"A nation mighty and conquering" — the United States has been significantly victorious in all its wars.

"Whose land the rivers divide" — what could be meant except the Mississippi and Missouri Rivers?

This kind of interpretation, which certainly has no standing in the world of scholarship, was yet impressive to my inquirer, particularly because it appealed to the Hebrew. I replied to him that the Hebrew word translated as "beyond" means "on the other side" and does indeed mean "west" in nine instances in the Old Testament. But in thirty-six instances it means "east." In such a phrase as "beyond the Jordan," it depends on where the writer imagines himself to be standing. As to the "water-drinking vessels," the Hebrew word for "papyrus" does indeed mean "that which drinks," since this reed grows in marshes. But the phrase is also used elsewhere. The mother of the infant Moses is said to have brought "for him a basket made of bulrushes" (Ex. 2:3) in which she floated him upon the Nile. Are we to understand from this that he journeyed up and down the river in a little steamboat? Isaiah's oracle is clearly designated as referring to Ethiopia. This, in his day, was a nation of some importance. Egypt was ruled for years by at least two Ethiopian dynasties. Should not the prophet be taken at his word? To identify his description with a twentieth-century country makes nonsense of what he had to say to his contemporaries.

So it is that an apparent show of knowledge can deceive honest people. Numerous equally extraordinary misinterpretations circulate among so-called " prophetic " groups. To reject this kind of interpretation is by no means to deny the significance of the prophets for our times; but this significance is of quite another sort, as we shall see.

THE SCOPE OF OUR STUDY

In order to consider what attitude we may take toward the matter of prediction and fulfillment in the Bible, and to discover what significance it may have for us, the plan of this book will be to examine a considerable number of such instances, and to try to determine the facts concerning them. We shall discover that the word " fulfill " has a variety of uses in Scripture and that it does not always mean the same thing. There are occasions where a mere similarity of words accounts for an alleged parallel. Other examples will show that no real prediction was involved in the passage cited, but that corresponding circumstances make a citation appropriate. Still others will show that the original prediction referred to a different event entirely, and that the similarity noted is incidental. Or, fulfillment may be in terms quite different from those implied and understood in the original statement. The New Testament usage is extremely varied in its application.

Likewise, our plan will be to examine more closely further examples of Old Testament predictions to determine what types they are. Some of them came to pass in Old Testament times; some did not. Many of them have not been realized up to the present day, and, since conditions have changed, there is small likelihood of their ever coming to pass. Perhaps the Christian will feel that some of these are at variance with the development of the Christian message, and that though they are in Scripture, they ought not to be fulfilled at all.

We shall also have to give some attention to what really is involved in prophecy, to what extent it is or is not predictive in character, and what its significance is for the modern day. Of necessity we must look at the so-called "false" prophets and try to distinguish the elements that make a seer to be called true or false. And, since fulfillment is claimed for passages from other parts of the Old Testament, especially The Psalms and the books of the Pentateuch, we shall consider the contributions that modern Biblical scholarship has made to the appreciation and understanding of these books, as well as to the books of the prophets, properly so called. It may be startling to some to discover that the New Testament quotes from the books of the Apocrypha, treating them as Scripture, though neither modern Judaism nor modern Protestantism considers them as having any special authority. We shall try to draw conclusions from the evidence and decide what is relevant to Christian faith today.

It is important to present-day Christians to come to a more precise understanding of the place of the Bible in Christian faith and life. The Protestant churches are built on a tradition, given prominence in Reformation and post-Reformation times, that the Bible is the standard authority on which to base belief and conduct. In rejecting an authoritative church, the Reformers made the Bible central. But in the centuries that followed, different circumstances have brought about profound changes in the way in which the book is regarded. The historical approach, to which we have referred, is partly responsible. Furthermore, the temper of our time, with its insistence on evidence and the relationship of cause to effect, brings into question some of the reasoning found in Scripture.

Nevertheless, the basic contention of the preachers and evangelists of New Testament times was that the gospel they proclaimed was indeed the fruition of Old Testament hopes and expectations. Therefore they drew upon the ancient heritage as often as they could, to show a continuity of faith. Their purpose was to show Jesus as the culmination of God's revelation of himself to men. In the words of the author of the Fourth Gospel, " Jesus did many other signs in the presence of the disciples, which are not written in this book; but these are written that you may believe that Jesus is the Christ, the Son of God, and that believing you may have life in his name " (John 20:30-31). It seems to have been this kind of purpose that brought about the selection and use of Old Testament predictions.

CHAPTER II

The Uses of Scripture

Wᴇ ʜᴀᴠᴇ ɴᴏᴛᴇᴅ that the writers of the Gospels go to great lengths to refer to things in the Old Testament that they claim to be fulfilled by events in the life of Christ. In fact, the impression seems to be produced that it is chiefly in events in the life of Jesus that the original statements have real significance. This or that circumstance is said to have come about "in order that the word of the prophet might be fulfilled." The uncritical mind may not find difficulty in such a statement; but one who thinks analytically in the patterns of contemporary life is not thus easily satisfied. Just what is meant by the use of the word "fulfill" under these circumstances? Does the word represent a reality, or does it belong to the category of conceptions that must be regarded as outmoded?

Tʜᴇ Usᴇ ᴏꜰ ᴛʜᴇ Oʟᴅ Tᴇsᴛᴀᴍᴇɴᴛ ɪɴ ᴛʜᴇ Gᴏsᴘᴇʟs

Fulfillment is a concept of quite varying connotations, depending on usage. The best way to make this clear may be to examine in some detail typical occasions in the Gospels where it is claimed. For example, it is said that Jesus went about healing the sick. Matthew explains:

This was to fulfil what was spoken by the prophet Isaiah:
"Behold, my servant whom I have chosen,
my beloved with whom my soul is well pleased.

I will put my Spirit upon him,
    and he shall proclaim justice to the Gentiles.
He will not wrangle or cry aloud,
    nor will any one hear his voice in the streets;
he will not break a bruised reed
    or quench a smoldering wick,
till he brings justice to victory;
    and in his name will the Gentiles hope."
                            (Matt. 12:17-21; Isa. 42:1-4.)

Now, this passage does not say anything about healing the sick. It does say of the servant of the Lord that he is one on whom is God's Spirit, who has a mission to the Gentiles, and whose method is not that of public display, but of quiet service. Therefore, according to Matthew, when Jesus went about healing the sick, this was in order to fulfill what Isaiah had said. But in what did fulfillment lie? Was it in the fact that the Spirit of God was on him? Or was it in some way a proclamation to the Gentiles? It does not appear that those who were healed were Gentiles. Or was the fulfillment in the manner of his work, which was unobtrusive? He had ordered those whom he healed not to make him known. Or did the fulfillment consist in his service to those who came to him, thereby putting new significance into the idea of serving others? It may be that it is unnecessary to decide. Matthew is not specific. The appropriateness of the quotation might be in any or all of these elements.

Matthew 2:13-15 tells of the flight of Joseph and Mary with the child Jesus into Egypt. This is said to have been because Joseph was warned in a dream that Herod was about to destroy the child. They remained in Egypt until Herod's death, and Matthew adds, " This was to fulfil what the Lord had spoken by the prophet, ' Out of Egypt have I called my son.' "

This verse is quoted from Hos. 11:1, in which Hosea speaks of the nation and of God's love for his people. Hosea says God treated the nation like a child:

> When Israel was a child, I loved him,
>   and out of Egypt I called my son.
> The more I called them,
>   the more they went from me;
>   . . . .
> Yet it was I who taught Ephraim to walk,
>   I took them up in my arms;
>   but they did not know that I healed them.
>
> (Hos. 11:1-3.)

The original reference here is to the exodus of Israel from Egypt in the days of Moses. Hosea pictures God, the Father of his people, leading them as one leads a child, teaching them along the way, even though they were perverse and sacrificed to foreign deities. In Ex. 4:22 the Lord is represented as referring to Israel as "my first-born son," and the metaphor is picked up by Hosea in fuller language. We note that there is no prediction indicated in Hosea's words. It is a historical reference so far as he is concerned. The idea that he was looking forward to Herod's time to forecast a later event is without Old Testament evidence. But Matthew notes an appropriate phrase and relates it to the situation he describes, claiming the one to be the fulfillment of the other.

Matthew then goes on to connect the slaughter of the innocents with a passage from Jeremiah. This is cited as a fulfillment of Jeremiah's words:

> A voice is heard in Ramah,
>   lamentation and bitter weeping.
> Rachel is weeping for her children;
>   she refuses to be comforted for her children,
>   because they are not.
>
> (Jer. 31:15.)

The original occasion of the prophet's words was the deportation of the inhabitants of Judah by Nebuchadrezzar (commonly called Nebuchadnezzar) in 597 B.C. Jeremiah pictures the exiles on their way to Babylon passing Rachel's tomb and envisions the ancestral mother grieving over what is happening to them. But the prophet consoles her:

> Keep your voice from weeping,
>   and your eyes from tears;
> for your work shall be rewarded,
>   says the Lord,
>
> and they shall come back from the land
>   of the enemy.
> There is hope for your future,
>   says the Lord,
>
> and your children shall come back to
>   their own country.
>   (Jer. 31:16-17.)

The basic message is therefore one of reassurance to the prophet's compatriots, embodying in a poetic form both the tragedy of the nation's fall and the hope and faith that one day it would be restored.

The location of the tomb of Rachel has been subject to ambiguity. Jeremiah's reference would clearly place it near Ramah, a few miles north of Jerusalem, as would the passage in I Sam. 10:2. According to Gen. 35:16-19, Rachel died when they were still some distance from Ephrath. This must, then, have been the name of a place north of Jerusalem. But the region south of Jerusalem was known as Ephrathah, and later tradition identified the location as one near Bethlehem, which accounts for the addition in Gen. 35:19 of " (that is, Bethlehem)." Drawing upon this later, erroneous tradition, Matthew connects Rachel's tomb with Bethlehem, and quotes Jeremiah, including the reference to Ramah, without explanation (Matt. 2:17-18), after having pointed to fulfillment in Herod's killing of the children in Bethlehem (v. 16).

In this instance we therefore have no anticipation of the later event by the earlier prophet. Rather, here is an apt phrase, not only made appropriate by the poetic ascription of grief to the reputed mother of the tribes of Israel over the misfortunes now come upon them but suited to Bethlehem because of the erroneous identification of the tomb site with that town. Matthew found in this combination of circumstances an agreement which he calls a fulfillment.

With respect to the birth of Jesus, Matthew records the appearance to Mary of an angel, who announces to her that she is to bear a son, whose name shall be Jesus, " for he will save his people from their sins." " Jesus " is the Greek form of the name " Joshua," which means " The Lord is salvation." Matthew adds,

All this took place to fulfil what the Lord had spoken by the prophet:
> " Behold, a virgin shall conceive and bear a son,
> and his name shall be called Emmanuel "
(which means, God with us).

(Matt. 1:22-23.)

Much discussion has centered on this passage, which is quoted from Isa. 7:14. The original prophecy was spoken by Isaiah to Ahaz in the crisis arising from the imminent invasion of Judah by Syria and Israel in the year 734 B.C. Isaiah counseled the king to take heed, to be quiet, and not to fear, for the prospective invasion would not succeed. Ahaz was vacillating, and the prophet added, " Ask a sign of the Lord your God." Ahaz did not want to ask for a sign, lest it commit him to a course of action he did not favor, so the prophet announced: " Therefore the Lord himself will give you a sign. Behold, a young woman shall conceive and bear a son, and shall call his name Immanuel. . . . For before the child knows how to refuse the evil and choose the good, the land before whose two kings you are in dread will be deserted."

There is general agreement among Old Testament scholars that the reference is to an anticipated birth to occur within the experience of Ahaz. It was a sign that the coalition of Syria with the

Northern Kingdom would not succeed. How could a sign that would not appear for several hundred years be a portent to Ahaz? Therefore, students of this passage are not convinced that it is a representation of a Messianic king who would someday appear, but rather, of an immediately contemporary event. The young woman who is with child is for Isaiah a present personality. Moreover, the phrase in Hebrew, "the young woman pregnant and bearing" (the words are an adjective and a participle), parallels almost exactly the words used in the book of Genesis. Hagar had fled from home because Sarai persecuted her. It is then recorded that an angel of the Lord met her in the wilderness and said: "I will so greatly multiply your descendants that they cannot be numbered for multitude. . . . Behold, you are with child, and shall bear a son; you shall call his name Ishmael." (Gen. 16:10-11.)

A closer examination of the Hebrew text of the passage in Isaiah reveals that the phrase "shall call his name" is actually a feminine form of the verb: "you [feminine] shall call his name Immanuel." Since Isaiah was speaking to Ahaz in making this statement, it would have been inappropriate to use a feminine form of the verb unless it was not meant to apply to Ahaz. It is the same form used by the author of Genesis in the Hagar account. Words spoken by the mother at the time of a birth significantly influenced the naming of a child. It appears that what is here is a birth announcement in the usual form of words. The verse is equivalent to "a child is about to be born." His name, "God with us," might indicate either deliverance or judgment, or perhaps both. For the next chapter indicates that

"the Lord is bringing up against them the waters of the River, mighty and many, the king of Assyria and all his glory; and it will rise over all its channels and go over all its banks; and it will sweep on into Judah, it will overflow and pass on, reaching even to the neck; and its outspread wings will fill the breadth of your land, O Immanuel."

> . . . .
> Take counsel together, but it will
>   come to nought;
> speak a word, but it will not stand,
> *for God is with us.*
>   (Isa. 8:7-8, 10, italics added.)

What the child signified to Ahaz was therefore the coming of God to deliver Judah from the present threat by Syria and Israel, and to judge by the more significant coming of the Assyrians who followed. This is the background of the passage quoted by Matthew. The fact that the Greek translation known to him used the word "virgin" to translate "young woman" may have seemed of special significance to the evangelist; but if so, his emphasis is on a matter of secondary importance so far as the original passage is concerned. If Matthew intended the emphasis to be upon the name Immanuel, this would be far more meaningful, although this is the only place in the New Testament where the name is connected with Jesus. In view of the intricacy of the problems that surround the interpretation of this passage in the Old Testament, it is precarious to make it a point of major importance so far as Matthew is concerned. Yet this very intricacy is important to us as we consider the subject at hand.

Matthew was acquainted with a current Jewish interpretation that connected the expected Messiah with the town of Bethlehem. He quotes Micah 5:2, which reads as follows:

> But you, O Bethlehem Ephrathah,
>   who are little to be among the clans of Judah,
> from you shall come forth for me
>   one who is to be ruler in Israel,
> whose origin is from of old,
>   from ancient days.

Actually, this is not necessarily a statement concerning the place of the Messiah's birth, but a reference to his lineage. He is represented as from the line of David. Other passages of the Old Testament refer to Jerusalem as "the city of David," but the mention of Bethlehem places the emphasis here not upon David the king, or David the warrior, but upon David the shepherd, chosen from among the sons of Jesse to become ruler. It calls attention to his origin among his people, from a relatively obscure village.

But Matthew sees in the birth of Jesus an event that makes the town of Bethlehem much more significant. He therefore quotes Micah freely, paraphrasing the ancient prophecy, and, indeed, altering its sense. Bethlehem, far from being obscure in Matthew's eyes, now assumes great importance. He therefore makes the quotation read:

> And you, O Bethlehem, in the land of Judah,
> are by no means least among the rulers of Judah;
> for from you shall come a ruler
> who will govern my people Israel.
>
> (Matt. 2:6.)

Instead of being an unimportant village, Bethlehem is "by no means least" among Judah's towns. Jesus, now recognized as the Messiah, not only is connected with David's lineage but also enhances the status of the town from which his illustrious predecessor came. The evangelist thus holds himself free to quote quite casually in support of his contentions.

The same is true of Matthew's reference to John the Baptist. John is said to have been preaching in the wilderness, "Repent, for the kingdom of heaven is at hand." Matthew then explains:

> This is he who was spoken of by the prophet Isaiah when he said,
> "The voice of one crying in the wilderness:
> Prepare the way of the Lord,
> make his paths straight."
>
> (Matt. 3:1-3.)

Yet The Book of Isaiah, in the fortieth chapter, does not actually speak of a voice in the wilderness, but rather, of a road across the desert. The passage is poetry, and one of the characteristics of Hebrew poetry is parallelism in structure. A first line makes a statement, which is repeated or amplified in a second line. Sometimes the second line states the opposite of the first. In the passage under examination, the second line repeats the first in alternate words.

> A voice cries:
> "In the wilderness prepare the way of the Lord,
>   make straight in the desert a highway for our God."
> (Isa. 40:3.)

The fact that three of the Gospels refer to the voice crying in the wilderness points to the probability that the early church commonly quoted the Old Testament reference in this way, adapting it as a validation of John's preaching, anticipating the appearance of Christ and his message.

Upon returning from Egypt, Joseph, it is recorded, settled in Galilee, in the town of Nazareth. Matthew says that this was in order "that what was spoken by the prophets might be fulfilled, 'He shall be called a Nazarene'" (Matt. 2:23). There is no specific Old Testament passage in which mention is made of a Nazarene. In ancient times, men who took certain vows were called Nazirites, but the reference is not to this. The word is not grammatically connected with Nazareth, and Jesus was not a Nazirite in the Biblical sense. It seems that most likely Matthew is here making use of a play upon words, for the Hebrew term *netser* is the word for "branch" or "sprout," used with reference to the hoped-for Messianic king in Isa. 11:1:

> There shall come forth a shoot from the stump of Jesse,
>   and a branch shall grow out of his roots.

In recognizing Jesus as the Messiah, Matthew not only sees a fulfillment of this Old Testament hope but even finds in the word itself an anticipation of Nazareth as the place where he should be brought up.

Another instructive example of the way in which the Gospels understand fulfillment is found in the record of the thirty pieces of silver paid to Judas for his betrayal of Jesus (Matt. 27:3-10). It is said that Judas threw down the money in the Temple, but that the priests, regarding it as blood money, considered it unlawful to be put into the treasury. Instead, they used it to buy a burial place known as the Field of Blood, popularly referred to as the potter's field. This is said to be a fulfillment of what had been spoken by the prophet Jeremiah. The reference is more properly to a passage in Zech. 11:12-13 in which that prophet is figuratively paid his wages, thirty shekels of silver, which he takes and casts into the treasury in the house of the Lord. The Hebrew word for " treasury " (*otsar*) was subsequently corrupted by a minor change into the word for " potter " (*yotser*), which is the present reading of the text. It is apparent, however, that " treasury " is correct. Matthew brings into his reference both ideas, that of treasury and that of potter, freely paraphrasing and adding reminiscences of Jeremiah's visit to the potter's house (Jer. 18:1-3), and of his purchase of a field from Hanamel, his cousin (ch. 32:6-15). Matthew then ascribes the entire paraphrase to Jeremiah and points to its fulfillment in the circumstances connected with Judas' betrayal money. The passage cited as fulfilled is thus composite, arranged by Matthew or his sources.

Let us note one further example of fulfillment, in the accounts of the Palm Sunday entrance of Jesus into Jerusalem. All four of the Gospels record how Jesus entered the city riding upon a colt. This was seen as a fulfillment of Zech. 9:9:

> Rejoice greatly, O daughter of Zion!
>   Shout aloud, O daughter of Jerusalem!
> Lo, your king comes to you;
>   triumphant and victorious is he,

> humble and riding on an ass,
> on a colt the foal of an ass.

This passage had long been regarded as characterizing the Messianic king by calling attention to the peace resulting from his victories. The editor of the Gospel of Matthew failed to recognize the poetic parallelism in Zechariah, in which the ass and the colt are two references to the same animal. The poetry repeats the idea, saying the same thing twice. But Matthew introduces into his account both an ass and a colt, indicating that the Master rode both of the animals, thus fulfilling the prophecy (Matt. 21:1-7). Quite apart from the impossibility of riding two animals at once, let it be added that the alleged fulfillment is in no way dependent upon this circumstance. Yet we are struck with the fact that the First Gospel was at pains to introduce the second animal in order to assure, as completely as possible, the fulfillment of the passage in Zechariah.

It will be seen from the foregoing instances that the usage of the Gospels is, in a considerable number of cases, open to disturbing questions on the part of the twentieth-century reader. What may have seemed convincing in an earlier generation gives rise to doubtful queries in our day. Can it be that prediction did not really take place and that what is alleged as fulfillment may turn out to be nothing more than literary comparison? Or is there something more basic in all of this than the simple equation of a New Testament event with an Old Testament reference that seems appropriate? With these questions in mind, let us turn our attention to the preaching of the apostles, and the usage of the early church.

The Use of the Old Testament by the Early Church

Three stages may be discerned in the growth of the Christian community. Those who were attracted to Jesus and who acknowledged him as Lord were, in the first instance, all Jews. They accepted their heritage and were conscientious in the observance of the obligations it laid upon them. They heard Jesus gladly and called him "Rabbi," "teacher." He taught with authority, yet they appreciated the fact that his instruction was not in the dogmatic manner of the scribes. They saw him as seeking the spirit rather than the letter of Moses and the prophets. In fact, they hailed him as a prophet, in line with the great teachers of the past. They understood that he was in the continuity of the faith they had known.

Yet there was something distinctive about "the Way," as they termed it. The incisive insights with which he interpreted the heritage they had in common brought them to recognize his uniqueness, and the freshness of his approach to the ancient faith was appealing. After his death and resurrection they were ready to risk all in order to follow him, for they believed in the abundant life he had promised them.

Under the influence of Paul and others, it presently was seen that this abundant life was available to those whose heritage was not Jewish. A mission to the Gentiles was undertaken, and before long the followers of "the Way" included a considerable number of persons who had not come up through the Jewish faith.

Hence the question arose: Must one first become a Jew in order to be a follower of the Lord? Some asserted that this was the case; but at the conference in Jerusalem about twenty years after the crucifixion, the matter was debated (Acts, ch. 15) and the decision was reached that it was not necessary to observe the law of Moses in order to be a follower of Christ. A second stage therefore evolved, in which some members of the Christian community were Jews and some were Gentiles. It was not necessary to become a Jew in order to be a Christian.

Eventually a third stage emerged, in which it became apparent that a choice must be made. One must regard himself either as a follower of the law or as an adherent of the church. It appeared that fully to obey the law would hinder complete allegiance to Christ. Various elements may have contributed to this development. One was the revolt of Palestinian Jews against Rome that brought about the destruction of Jerusalem by Titus in A.D. 70. More important was the increasing number of Christian churches in the Roman world; these were made up of converts whose outlook was broadly inclusive of the far horizons of the Roman Empire and who would be impatient of meticulous observances of legalism. The church in Jerusalem no doubt continued to be looked to for guidance, but the weight of Christian witness shifted to the Gentile world. Exactly when the final identification of Christianity as a new religion instead of as a Jewish sect took place is hard to say. It may have come about in the second or third century of the Christian era. In any case, it probably did not take place before the New Testament was completed. Since the church began among those whose heritage was Jewish, there was a natural conviction among them that " the Way " was not contrary to what they had always held but was in fact the means of making that heritage more meaningful. They therefore sought evidence that would prove the continuity of one with the other. This would be especially true of the church in Jerusalem, which, at least in the earlier stages, must have been almost entirely composed of Jews. But in the churches established in other parts of the Empire, the number of members of non-Jewish origin tended to increase. Therefore Paul emphasized, in writing to the Romans, that the gospel " is the power of God for salvation to every one who has faith, to the Jew first and also to the Greek " (Rom. 1:16). Again and again the church pointed to the promises held to have been made originally to Abraham, but finding fuller expression throughout Israel's history, and took the position that these promises were now viewed as available to all, whether Jew or Gentile. As Paul wrote to the Christians in Asia Minor: " So then, those who are men of faith are blessed with Abraham who had faith." (Gal. 3:9.) For Paul, it was chiefly a matter of faith, centered in Christ. " And if you are Christ's, then you are Abraham's offspring, heirs according to promise." (V. 29.)

The abundant life is consequently seen to be the fruition of all that God has made available to men. Yet it was not necessary to start anew in the discovery of God's providence. The church looked to the past to determine the lines along which men had come to the present hour. They believed that the divine purpose had been seen through the years; now it was coming into its own. They therefore linked the present with the past, convinced that what was new was indeed in line with what was old.

Ever since the Kingdoms of Israel and Judah had fallen, a succession of foreign empires had exercised sovereignty over the land of Palestine. The conquests of Alexander the Great, accomplished between 334 and 323 B.C., resulted in the spread of Greek culture to the Middle East. This cultural penetration continued under the so-called Hellenistic kingdoms that followed Alexander, and it began to be apparent that changes in thought and custom affected many Jews. The party known as Sadducees favored including in Judaism the best of Greek thought and custom. On the other hand, those who called themselves Pharisees laid great stress on maintaining the traditional Jewish way of life. The Pharisees therefore undertook to promote careful observance of the traditional law, in order to preserve the purity of the people and their faith. Hope still prevailed that Israel's ancient independence might be restored. A national resurgence was longed for. At least one small minority party, known as Zealots, favored direct military action in order to restore the ancient glory of the people. The actual future of Judaism in the first century was not at all certain.

In this kind of atmosphere the first Christians thought of the Kingdom of God, not as a national kingdom, but as one embracing other nations as well. It could well be a universal dominion in which all might share. The idea that God had chosen a people for himself was understood not to lead to the restoration of national independence, but rather, to the inclusion in the kingdom of representatives of many nations who would believe and follow Christ. They conceived of the Christian Way not as an offshoot of the faith of their fathers, but rather, as its continuation and fruition.

Specifically, they attempted to prove that the goals set forth in the Law and the Prophets were now in fact at the point of realization in the gospel of their Lord. In answer to Pilate's question, Jesus had replied, "My kingship is not of this world" (John 18:36). By this he did not mean that his Kingdom was not in this world, for it was and is, but rather, that his was not to be a worldly kingdom in character. The early church therefore searched the Scriptures to discover evidence of the authentic nature of its faith.

THE PREACHING OF THE APOSTLES

The first recorded preaching of the risen Lord is found in the account of Pentecost, in the second chapter of The Acts. The apostles realized that a proclamation of the faith must now be made, and Peter is said to have claimed that the fact that the apostles were filled with God's Holy Spirit was the realization of a prophecy of Joel:

> And in the last days it shall be, God declares,
> that I will pour out my Spirit upon all flesh,
> and your sons and daughters shall prophesy,
> and your young men shall see visions,
> and your old men shall dream dreams;
> yea, and on my menservants and my maidservants
>   in those days
> I will pour out my Spirit; and they shall prophesy.
> (Acts 2:17-18; Joel 2:28-29.)

The original prophecy of Joel was a poetic description of the Day of the Lord, what we might call the Last Judgment. But Peter, picking up the phrase "pour out my Spirit," finds that the Pentecost experience involves exactly that; therefore he appropriately quotes the prophet and indicates that what has now occurred is that of which the prophet spoke. Peter does not claim that now is the Day of the Lord. He makes no parallel with the part of the passage that mentions wonders in heaven and signs on earth, "blood and fire and columns of smoke." The pouring out of God's Spirit is sufficient for him to claim that what the prophet stated has now been realized.

This pattern seems to have been characteristic of the early preaching of the church. Jesus is said to have been "delivered up according to the definite plan and foreknowledge of God" (Acts 2:23). Peter quotes two separate psalms: "Thou wilt not abandon my soul to Hades, nor let thy Holy One see corruption" (Acts 2:27; Ps. 16:10) and "The Lord said to my Lord, Sit at my right hand, till I make thy enemies a stool for thy feet" (Acts 2:34-35; Ps. 110:1). The original psalms in both cases seem to have had other reference, but the phrases are appropriate to the message that Peter sets forth.

In another proclamation to the people, Peter said, "What God foretold by the mouth of all the prophets, that his Christ should suffer, he thus fulfilled" (Acts 3:18). Later in the same address he continued: "Moses said, 'The Lord God will raise up for you a prophet from your brethren as he raised me up. You shall listen to him.'" (Acts 3:22.)

We may note that not "all the prophets" speak of a suffering Messiah; no doubt this reference is to the Servant in Isa., ch. 53. However, the "prophet from your brethren" (Deut. 18:15-16) indicated a succession of men in the prophetic office who would follow Moses and, like him, be God's spokesmen to the people. Peter finds in these passages a further likeness to the career of the Lord.

In I Cor. 15:3-5, Paul reminds his readers of the gospel he had preached to them: "That Christ died for our sins in accordance with the scriptures, that he was buried, that he was raised on the third day in accordance with the scriptures, and that he appeared to Cephas . . ." Here, again, it is apparent that the apostolic message included reference to the Scriptures in order to show that the death and resurrection of the Lord, and his subsequent glorification, were in line with ancient tradition.

At Antioch of Pisidia, Paul attended a synagogue service. After the reading of the Law and the Prophets, in response to the invitation of the rulers of the synagogue for exhortation from any present, he made bold to arise and preach Jesus as the Christ. He began by relating the history of Israel: the providence of God for a people whom he had chosen, his deliverance of them from Egypt, their conquest and settlement in Canaan, the rise of the house of David. He directly linked the coming of Jesus to this sequence as its latest development, indicating that his deliverance to death was because their rulers " did not recognize him nor understand the utterances of the prophets which are read every sabbath " and " fulfilled these by condemning him " (Acts 13:15-27). Then he continued, "We bring you the good news that what God promised to the fathers, this he has fulfilled to us their children by raising Jesus " (vs. 32-33), and quoted two psalms and paraphrased a passage in Isaiah:

> Thou art my Son,
> today I have begotten thee.
> . . . .
> I will give you the holy and sure blessings of David.
> . . . .
> Thou wilt not let thy Holy One see corruption.
> (Acts 13:32-35; Ps. 2:7; Isa. 55:3; Ps. 16:10.)

It is apparent that the whole statement was intended to show the continuity of the work of Christ with the history of God's people Israel.

THE TESTIMONIES

The foregoing instances seem to indicate a pattern in New Testament proclamation that was followed not only by Peter and Paul but by the apostolic preachers generally. Regularly these preachers referred to the Old Testament for source material to illustrate and prove that Jesus is the center of the same faith that they and their fathers have always held. It is noteworthy, too, that combinations of passages from different parts of the Scriptures are frequently linked together and are used in such combination by more than one writer of the New Testament. This points to a usage that seems to have prevailed in the church of the earliest years, in which there was a tradition that specific Old Testament passages could be used to support various aspects of Christian belief.

It looks, therefore, as though the use of the Old Testament in this way is earlier than the preaching of Paul or the writing of any of the New Testament books. These are an exhibition of a method of interpretation that had already established itself. In the middle of the third century one of the church fathers, Cyprian, bishop of Carthage, prepared a document entitled " Testimonia " (" Testimonies "), which contained a collection of Old Testament passages organized and classified for use by Christian teachers and preachers. It is quite plausible, however, that Cyprian was not originating something but was acting as an editor, putting into comprehensive and usable form a collection of passages that had previously been brought together and had, in fact, originated in the earliest days of the church. Scholars recognize that Tertullian, Irenaeus, and Justin, who preceded Cyprian, evidently had access to some such similar lists. How far back they go can only be guessed, but the New Testament evidence would seem to indicate that they antedated both the Gospels and the epistles.

Additional evidence for such early collections of " testimonies " may be recognized in the following facts:

1. Certain Old Testament passages are quoted by more than one New Testament writer. It appears, therefore, that these were probably not original with the several authors but were already known and used as common illustrations of elements in the proclamation of the gospel.

2. Very often the wording of a quotation does not follow closely the original in the Old Testament. A Greek version called the Septuagint is usually followed, since it was well known, but the rendering differs frequently from this as well. Nevertheless, New Testament writers often agree closely with each other in

the divergent wording, suggesting that the variant had been used before in this form and may have been traditional in the Christian community.

3. Some quotations combine elements from two or more Old Testament sources, and the combined unit is treated as one quotation. This suggests that the combination may have existed previously in the tradition of the church. Such an instance is seen in Mark 1:2-3, where the source is indicated only as Isaiah, though Malachi's words are included. Perhaps this is also the case with Matthew's reference to the thirty pieces of silver, quoted from Zechariah but including allusions from Jeremiah, who is then indicated as the source fulfilled.

4. Passages connected by some characteristic word or idea tend to be grouped together, though they may have little else in common — for example, verses that mention a stone: the stone rejected by the builders, the cornerstone of Zion, the stone of stumbling, and the stone that destroyed the image in the vision of Daniel.

If quotations were made by New Testament writers from an already existing collection or tradition, it would account for verbal variations, citations from the wrong prophet, and parallels in application. We are therefore dealing with a custom that prevailed widely in the apostolic age and that assumed definite patterns recognized as legitimate and proper in the support of the teaching of the early church. Each pattern became familiar by use, and the entire process was evidently considered as fitting into the formula of prediction and fulfillment. As modern students, we may be inclined to skepticism about the legitimacy of some of these uses. What we must do is to see them in the perspective of modern scholarship, but at the same time to recognize in them the features that commended them to the early church for its missionary use.

It therefore appears that during the first two decades after the resurrection of the Lord, Christian preachers systematically drew from the Old Testament a variety of passages that were gener-

ally accepted as anticipating Christ or validating the gospel in
Old Testament terms. They were intended to show that " the
Way " was the same as that which was described by psalmist,
poet, and prophet in former years. Passages were sometimes
strung together like a chain; usually they had related originally
to entirely different subject matter from the context in which the
Christian preachers applied them. But the one thing they had in
common was the great tradition that God had redeemed his people in times past and had promised to continue to be their Redeemer in days to come. The purpose of the quotations was to
show that the good news was not an intrusion into Israel's history but was in continuity with it; and that the gospel of Christ
was, in fact, the logical and necessary outcome of hopes long implanted within the national consciousness.

The Use of the Old Testament by Jesus

Since the earliest preaching of the apostles included the use of
the Old Testament as verification of their message, is it possible
that they were doing something that had in fact been originated
by Jesus himself? They were convinced that the gospel they
preached, although based on events that had only recently taken
place, was in fact part of the continuity of the past. The ancient
promise that God would be the redeemer and savior of his people was now held to take on new meaning in the person of our
Lord. But it was, in their understanding, the same promise. Had
they learned this understanding from Jesus himself? What was
his attitude toward the Scriptures?

We must, of course, keep in mind that we see the preaching
and teaching of Jesus through the eyes of the apostles and the
writers of the Gospels. No doubt his reported sayings have been
preserved in the forms in which they were remembered and
passed on by the oral tradition of the church. But there is uni-
form testimony that Jesus connected what he had to say with the
heritage of the past and understood that he was making explicit
what should have been apprehended by thoughtful and intelli-

gent observers of that heritage.

Luke records the beginning of the public ministry of Jesus as occurring in the synagogue at Nazareth. It was the Sabbath Day, and Jesus stood up to read the appointed Scripture. The passage was this (Isa. 61:1-2a):

> "The Spirit of the Lord is upon me,
> because he has anointed me to preach good
>   news to the poor.
> He has sent me to proclaim release to
>   the captives
> and recovering of sight to the blind,
> to set at liberty those who are oppressed,
> to proclaim the acceptable year of the Lord."

And he closed the book, and gave it back to the attendant, and sat down; and the eyes of all in the synagogue were fixed on him. And he began to say to them, "Today this scripture has been fulfilled in your hearing." (Luke 4:18-21.)

What he read was the sixty-first chapter of Isaiah, and it is very probable that it was not simply the two verses quoted here, but the entire reading section for the day. These key words identify the passage. It would be quite unwarranted to suppose, as some have proposed, that Jesus ended his reading with the words last quoted, deliberately omitting the words immediately following: "And the day of vengeance of our God."

The content of the passage deals with the working of God's Spirit through the prophet, to reassure his hearers of divine favor to them. Those who are afflicted, in captivity, in mourning, or otherwise depressed are reminded that God's grace will permit them to surmount their difficulties and enable them to rise above present circumstances. What did Jesus mean when he told those who were in the synagogue that "this scripture" had been fulfilled in their hearing? He meant that the same Spirit of God who through long generations had been working in the hearts of men was present in Nazareth, once again exhibiting that same power.

The release spoken of by the prophet was currently available, under new circumstances, and the ministry that was now beginning was a new exhibition of the power of God to meet the needs of men. The ancient words spoke afresh to the contemporary scene. Surely the prophet did not have Nazareth in mind when he spoke or wrote the original passage. But a new appropriateness had now been sensed, and it was significantly called by Jesus a fulfillment of the prophet's words. He went on to explain what this meant in the new day, and adduced further illustrations from the activities of Elijah and Elisha; but his hearers were unwilling to accept this interpretation, and rejected him. Thus did Jesus connect his new mission with the ancient truth.

Nevertheless, he felt at liberty to reinterpret the tradition of the past. In speaking to the multitudes on the mountain, Jesus is reported to have said, " Think not that I have come to abolish the law and the prophets; I have come not to abolish them but to fulfil them " (Matt. 5:17). There can be no reasonable doubt that this recorded saying affords a clue to his purpose and attitude throughout his ministry. Yet he was not bound by the letter of the law. He called attention to statements found in the law and extended their application. " You have heard that it was said to the men of old, ' You shall not kill; and whoever kills shall be liable to judgment.' But I say to you that every one who is angry with his brother shall be liable to judgment." (Matt. 5:21-22.) Thus he emphasized that attention should be given not alone to outward act, but to inner emotion or intention which is significant as leading to external deed. He continued: " So if you are offering your gift at the altar, and there remember that your brother has something against you, leave your gift there before the altar and go; first be reconciled to your brother, and then come and offer your gift." (Vs. 23-24.)

Others of the commandments are similarly referred to. "You have heard that it was said, ' You shall not commit adultery.' But I say to you that every one who looks at a woman lustfully has already committed adultery with her in his heart." (Vs. 27-28.)

Or, "Again you have heard that it was said to the men of old, 'You shall not swear falsely, but shall perform to the Lord what you have sworn.' But I say to you, Do not swear at all, either by heaven, for it is the throne of God, or by the earth, for it is his footstool, or by Jerusalem, for it is the city of the great King. And do not swear by your head, for you cannot make one hair white or black. Let what you say be simply 'Yes' or 'No'; anything more than this comes from evil." (Vs. 33-37.)

With reference to the Old Testament law of retaliation, "An eye for an eye, a tooth for a tooth," Jesus taught turning the other cheek, or going a second mile. According to him, an attitude of concern toward others, rather than of retaliation, should determine action. It is therefore clear that Jesus was no legalist. If he respected Old Testament law, it was not in any slavish way, but in an attitude that carried the principle far beyond the mere letter of what was said. This is in part what he meant by "fulfil."

On another occasion, recorded in the thirteenth chapter of Matthew, Jesus is said to have been asked the question, "Why do you speak to them in parables?" His recorded reply is:

To you it has been given to know the secrets of the kingdom of heaven, but to them it has not been given. . . . With them indeed is fulfilled the prophecy of Isaiah which says:
> "You shall indeed hear but never understand,
>   and you shall indeed see but never perceive.
> For this people's heart has grown dull,
>   and their ears are heavy of hearing,
>   and their eyes they have closed,
> lest they should perceive with their eyes,
>   and hear with their ears,
> and understand with their heart,
>   and turn for me to heal them."

Blessed are your eyes, for they see, and your ears, for they hear. (Matt. 13:10-11, 14-16.)

With these listeners who were not able to understand was repeated what Isaiah had said about his contemporaries, whose eyes
were also closed and whose ears were stopped. Isaiah's description was of the men of his time, who did not comprehend what
he was saying to them. The application made by Jesus was that
a repetition of this situation confronted him also: his hearers had
the same kind of insensitivity. It is unnecessary to believe that
Isaiah was foretelling a situation in the Christian era. Rather,
here was another instance of lack of response, and Jesus indicated that the words of Isaiah were thus fulfilled.

Jesus correctly noted that the teaching of the Old Testament
had often been obscured by generations of Rabbinic tradition. Ancient regulations had become subject to interpretation and reinterpretation to such an extent that the original intent was in
many instances completely overlooked. Jesus called attention to
this when the Pharisees and scribes asked why his disciples seemed
to be lax with respect to washing the hands in accordance with
"the tradition of the elders." His reply was that his inquirers
were guilty of a greater laxity; he pointed to a custom called
"corban," whereby a person could assign or give to God such of
his property as he might designate, and directed attention to a
misuse of this principle when a son sought thus to avoid sharing
his possessions with needy parents. Yet the commandment stated,
"Honor your father and your mother." He said, "You have a fine
way of rejecting the commandment of God, in order to keep your
tradition!" For further emphasis he quoted Isaiah:

Well did Isaiah prophesy of you hypocrites, as it is written,
> "This people honors me with their lips,
> but their heart is far from me;
> in vain do they worship me,
> teaching as doctrines the precepts of men."
(Mark 7:6-7, quoting freely from Isa. 29:13.)

Seeing in this passage, addressed originally to Israel, an appropriateness to the situation at hand, Jesus made it specific by the words

" prophesy of you." Whenever men put human regulations above the ethical requirement of true religion, the prophet might be said to speak " of you."

In connection with the series of parables related by Jesus concerning the Kingdom of Heaven, it is noted that Jesus " said nothing to them without a parable." Matthew explains:

> This was to fulfil what was spoken by the prophet:
> " I will open my mouth in parables,
> I will utter what has been hidden
> since the foundation of the world."
> (Matt. 13:34-35.)

This is a quotation from Ps. 78:2, preceding a lengthy account of the history of Israel and the lessons that should be drawn from it. The Hebrew word translated " parable " really means a saying, or even a riddle, rather than an apt story for purposes of illustration. In this verse it designates a wisdom poem, marked by parallelism. The Greek or Aramaic translation known to Matthew suggested the idea of parable, and therefore Matthew considered it appropriate for quotation with reference to the illustrative parables of Jesus. Hence he could say that the practice of Jesus fulfilled the psalm, though in fact the correspondence of the two is really dependent upon a kind of wordplay. Surely there is no prediction that came to pass. Fulfillment must be seen to have a much wider use in Scripture than realization of a forecast.

In the instance of the " sign of Jonah " we have an instructive variant, but without the use of the word " fulfil." According to Matthew, some of the scribes and Pharisees came and said to Jesus, " Teacher, we wish to see a sign from you." He replied: " No sign shall be given . . . except the sign of the prophet Jonah. For as Jonah was three days and three nights in the belly of the whale, so will the Son of man be three days and three nights in the heart of the earth. The men of Nineveh will arise at the judgment with this generation and condemn it; for they repented at the preaching of Jonah, and behold, something greater than Jonah is here.

The queen of the South will arise at the judgment with this generation and condemn it; for she came from the ends of the earth
to hear the wisdom of Solomon, and behold, something greater
than Solomon is here." (Matt. 12:38-42.)

Exactly what is the sign of Jonah? Many will say it is the three
days and three nights, thus forecasting the death of Jesus. But in
the parallel passage in Luke, there is no mention of the three days
and three nights. Instead, Luke records, as does Matthew, that the
men of Nineveh repented at Jonah's preaching and that the
Queen of Sheba recognized Solomon's wisdom when she encountered it. The sign, therefore, is in Nineveh's repentance and in the
admiration of the Queen of Sheba, unless Luke missed the point
to the illustration, which is improbable. The sign is not in the
three days and three nights, which evidently is a further addition
by Matthew. The point to the sign is that the teaching of Jesus
should no more need external authentication to be believed than
did Jonah's preaching or Solomon's wisdom; it commends itself
as valid to those who are ready to comprehend, and no further
sign of verification should be necessary for intelligent hearers.

On a notable occasion, Jesus cast out the money changers from
the Temple and said, " It is written, ' My house shall be called a
house of prayer '; but you make it a den of robbers " (Matt. 21:12-
13). He was quoting Isa. 56:7; but he repeated, without attribut-
ing it to its source, Jeremiah's comment (Jer. 7:11) about the
Temple as a den of robbers. Jesus referred to the trading, no doubt
sometimes dishonest, that took place in the Temple; but Jeremiah's original statement had nothing to do with conducting busi-
ness in the sanctuary. Rather, Jeremiah referred to the people of
his day as being so satisfied with the glorious house of the Lord,
assuming that its presence proved their faithfulness and righteousness, that they would steal, murder, and do all kinds of evil, and
then come and stand in the Temple and say, " We are forgiven."
The " den of robbers " in Jeremiah's use meant a robbers' lair, a
refuge to which they supposed they might retreat in safety. When
Jesus used the phrase, it had a different content, being applied to

merchandising in the sanctuary.

The use that Jesus made of the Old Testament, if we may trust these examples, was therefore partly illustrative and partly didactic. He intended by his quotations to teach his hearers. In none of these instances did Jesus remotely indicate that the Old Testament prophet had predicted what would occur in New Testament times. Rather, he found in his own day prevailing attitudes and outlooks that could be illustrated from Old Testament incidents and references. His characterization of his contemporaries was made more vivid, and was given historical reference, by mention of passages of Scripture with which his listeners were familiar. His use makes the matter of fulfillment quite different from what it would have been had he claimed that the prophet foresaw what should one day occur and described it minutely in terms that were later to be realized in concrete fact.

Having now observed typical instances of the use of Scripture by the writers of the Gospels, by the preachers of the early church, and by Jesus himself, we are in a position to attempt a more comprehensive definition of what is involved in prediction and fulfillment. Such fulfillment rests primarily on the character of what is quoted. Since the sources cited were understood by the speaker or writer, as well as by his audience, as having more than ordinary interest and significance, and since they are often referred to as Scripture, let us turn our attention to the way in which this body of material had come into being, and to how it was regarded by the early church, and why.

CHAPTER III

The Accumulation of Hebrew Scripture

THE MANNER in which the New Testament writers make use of quotations from the Old Testament assumes that the citations made have specific and unique authority. They belonged, indeed, to the history of the Jewish people; however, they were not cited primarily because they were old, but because they were of peculiar significance. They were authoritative Scripture. In order to appreciate this fact, we should take account of the process by which they received such recognition.

The terms are varied in which reference is made by the New Testament writers. The second letter to Timothy states: " All scripture is inspired by God and profitable for teaching, for reproof, for correction, and for training in righteousness, that the man of God may be complete, equipped for every good work." (II Tim. 3:16-17.) Here the term is in the singular: " scripture " (*graphē*), as also in John 2:22 and Acts 8:32. It appears in the plural as " the scriptures " (*hai graphai*) in Mark 12:24 and I Cor. 15:3-4. The phrase " holy scriptures " (*hagiai graphai*) is used in Rom. 1:2. A parallel usage is found when the books referred to are called " the writings " (*ta grammata*) (John 5:47) or " the sacred writings " (*ta hiera grammata*) (II Tim. 3:15). Sometimes when particular citations are made, the source is referred to as " the book " (*hē biblos* or *to biblion*), usually in combination with a more precise definition as to the kind of book, such as " the book of the law " (Gal. 3:10), " the book of Moses " (Mark

12:26), "the book of the words of Isaiah the prophet" (Luke 3:4), "the Book of Psalms" (Luke 20:42), or, in quoting Amos, "the book of the prophets" (Acts 7:42), seemingly referring to the Twelve Prophets that were considered as one book. The plural of the Greek word for "book" (*biblia*) is, of course, the origin of our English word "Bible."

In designating the sources of their quotations by such terms, the New Testament writers meant the Old Testament books as we have them. But there are allusions also to books not contained in the Protestant Bible. Quite a number of passages reflect use of what are known as the books of the Apocrypha. A few make use of works that are no part of any collection of Scripture, properly so called; and several quotations are given that do not appear in any existing work that has survived until our time, and whose source is therefore unknown. The Wisdom of Jesus the Son of Sirach, also known as Ecclesiasticus, is the background of James 1:9 and of Heb. 11:35-36; The Wisdom of Solomon seems to be connected with Eph. 6:11-13; Heb. 1:3; II Cor. 5:4; and Rom. 1:20-32. It may also be alluded to in Matt. 27:43. The Book of Enoch has never been recognized as authentic by any official sanction, yet Jude 14-15 quotes Enoch 1:9 verbatim: "It was also of these that Enoch in the seventh generation from Adam prophesied, saying, 'Behold, the Lord came with his holy myriads, to execute judgment on all, and to convict all the ungodly of all their deeds of ungodliness which they have committed in such an ungodly way, and of all the harsh things which ungodly sinners have spoken against him.'" Jude also seems to consider as authoritative the so-called Assumption of Moses, which was likewise never officially recognized as Scripture. In v. 9 he states that "when the archangel Michael, contending with the devil, disputed about the body of Moses, he did not presume to pronounce a reviling judgment about him, but said, 'The Lord rebuke you.'" James 4:5 reads: "Or do you suppose it is in vain that the scripture says, 'He yearns jealously over the spirit which he has made to dwell in us'?" but this quotation which is called

" scripture " is unidentifiable and otherwise unknown. The same is true of the passage quoted in Eph. 5:14, unless this may be considered to be a free paraphrase of Isa. 26:19 combined with Isa. 60:1. Luke 11:49-51a quotes from what is called " the Wisdom of God," evidently a work that has been lost, and this same passage lies behind Matt. 23:34-35.

The fact that the New Testament writers make such citations, ascribing to them unusual significance, makes it clear that they had a concept of authority in books that had come down from the past. With the exception of the passage just noted in Luke 11:49-51a, the Gospels make use of the books of the Old Testament as we know them. Probably this is because they originated in Palestine, and only the books recognized by the Jews of Palestine were known to them or considered as useful authorities. But Paul and other New Testament writers were acquainted with the translation of the Old Testament into the Greek language, which circulated among Jews in the Greek-speaking world outside Palestine and which contained a number of books not recognized by Palestinian Jews. It suggests, furthermore, that the exact definition of what should be regarded as Scripture had not yet been completely made. Let us therefore consider the steps by which the Biblical books become recognized as authoritative.

When the prophets attributed their message to divine inspiration, they described it as "the word of the Lord" that came to them. Their words were considered as having divine authority. Thus, the spoken word was what should be heeded, when given under such circumstances. In early times, especially in the Middle East, great emphasis was placed upon spoken words. A spoken blessing was considered effective in conferring the benefits which it described. Conversely, a spoken curse was to be feared because it was thought to bring about the evil results of which it spoke. So it was with the preaching of the prophets. Their spoken word was potent because divine authority was ascribed to it. How did such authority come to be transferred to a written page? And how did an authoritative collection come into being, which could be quoted as the New Testament writers do?

THE RECOGNITION OF DEUTERONOMY AS SCRIPTURE

Four stages in this development are discernible. The process began in the days of Josiah, king of Judah, in the seventh century before Christ. The oppressive rule of Assyria over Judah was relaxing, and there was a resurgence of both a spirit of nationalism and a consequent independence of religious expression. Because of this, renovation of the Temple in Jerusalem was undertaken. A narrative of this event is found in the twenty-second chapter of II Kings. During the process of clearing the Temple, Hilkiah the high priest said to Shaphan the secretary, "I have found the book of the law in the house of the Lord" (II Kings 22:8). This book was read to Josiah, who in consternation perceived that what was enjoined in it was not currently being observed. He instructed his officers to make inquiry of the Lord concerning the book and its contents. They consulted Huldah the prophetess; she verified the blessings and judgments set forth in the book and announced these as the word of the Lord. Here was the authentication of a written book by a spoken prophetic word. The result was that King Josiah proclaimed a religious reformation of nationwide scope, revolutionizing the manner of worship. The book was read to the people, and they joined their king in a covenant to perform all the words written in the book. Altars to idolatrous deities were thrown down, their priests were deposed, idolatrous symbols were abolished from the Temple precincts, high places dedicated to other gods were destroyed, mediums and wizards were abolished, and observance of the Feast of Passover was instituted, for "no such passover had been kept since the days of the judges who judged Israel, or during all the days of the kings of Israel or of the kings of Judah" (II Kings 23:22). In these reforms, it was the authority of a book which was being recognized. Here was something that might be called a divine word, equal in authority to the spoken word, performing the function that previously had characterized the utterance of a prophet.

Scholars are united in recognizing that the book thus found and made the basis of Josiah's reformation is what we now know as Deuteronomy. An analysis of the particular aspects of change that were undertaken reveals that this is the one part of the Pentateuch where all of them are brought together. It could not have been the entire Pentateuch, because the book was read in its entirety on three separate occasions. Accordingly, this significant event in Josiah's reign is termed the Deuteronomic Reformation.

It appears to modern scholarship that the book had its origin in Judah shortly before its discovery. Moses had long been regarded as speaking with prophetic authority, but no written work had preserved what he said. Oral tradition had been passed down through the generations, setting forth the content of Israel's understanding of its origin, and emphasizing the part played by the patriarchal ancestors and the significance of the departure of the people from Egypt. Some person imbued with the spirit of the great prophets of the eighth century B.C. evidently felt called upon to supply a message from the prophetic voice of Moses so that Moses would not be inferior to later prophets whose words were remembered. He therefore composed a work which reflects in considerable measure the ideals of the great prophets of the eighth century before Christ, and carried these back to the great prophetic founder of the nation. He reflects their doctrine of the unity and spirituality of God (Deut. 6:4-9), the concept of a covenant between God and his people (Deut. 4:31; 7:6-11), humanitarianism in social relations (Deut. 24:10, 17, 19, 21), the idea of individual responsibility announced by Jeremiah and later extended upon by Ezekiel (Deut. 24:16; Jer. 31:29-30; Ezek., ch. 18), the orderly worship of God, the continuing revelation of God's will through a succession of prophets (Deut. 18:15-22), and a warning against false prophets (Deut. 13:1-3). The spring Feast of Unleavened Bread had been long observed in the land, probably having been adopted from the Canaanites. To this feast was now added an extra day commemorating the deliverance from Egypt, and the whole eight days were designated as Passover. By placing these teachings in the mouth of

Moses, additional importance was attached to them, emphasizing the prophetic teaching through the years.

The book has the form of a sermon, or series of sermons, delivered by Moses, the contents being attributed to divine inspiration, as was appropriate to prophecy. It is really not law in an exact sense. Even the so-called legal sections in Deut., chs. 12 to 26, are not enactments, but an appeal to the people to observe such customs and procedures in their communal life as are consistent with a theology that places love toward God as a primary and governing principle and that recognizes the need for compassion and mercy in dealings with one's fellows. The good land which they inherited was the gift of God, who had also cared for them in the wilderness. They were the people of the Lord, not because they were more numerous than other peoples, but because the Lord had set his heart upon them and was keeping the oath which he had sworn to their fathers by entering into covenant with them. Blessings were promised to the nation if it lived in accordance with these principles; curses would be pronounced in judgment if it failed in this regard. It is a book of real insight and prophetic spirit.

The act of placing such a book in the Temple where it might be found has sometimes been termed a pious fraud, but such a designation is based upon a misunderstanding of the character of ancient writings. The modern attitude toward literary production, in which there is a personal pride in authorship and in which the rights of authors are recognized and protected, did not prevail in ancient times. Existing writings could be added to or altered without any thought of impropriety. This has occurred in a great number of instances in the Old Testament. The writer of the book found in the Temple was not dishonest. He was earnestly and conscientiously supplying what he considered to be a need, and he did it according to his understanding of what Moses and the prophets who followed him had come to believe to be the form and content of God's revelation to his people. The circumstances of the time of Moses he derived from the great national epics that set forth what the people remembered from the times of the patriarchal ancestors to the conquest of Canaan. For generations these had been passed on orally, but by his time they were no doubt to some considerable measure in writing as well.

The idea that there should be a book setting forth the words of Moses probably reflected the changing attitude toward prophetic utterances. The earliest prophets did not write books, so far as we know. They were dynamic men of action as well as word. Nathan, Ahijah, Elijah, Elisha, and their successors were remembered for what they did as well as what they said. But by the eighth century, the disciples of the prophets began to treasure written records of their utterances.

Isaiah may have had this in mind when he found that his listeners were unresponsive, hearing but not understanding, seeing but not perceiving. He would therefore let his message await a more opportune time. " Bind up the testimony, seal the teaching among my disciples. I will wait for the Lord, who is hiding his face from the house of Jacob, and I will hope in him." (Isa. 8:16-17.) Micah's message may have been preserved in writing, for a century later Jeremiah could quote the words that he had spoken concerning the prospective destruction of Jerusalem (Jer. 26:18). Jeremiah himself recorded that the word of the Lord instructed him to write in a book all the words that had been given to him to preach. (Jer. 30:1-2.) He further indicated divine direction to write on a scroll all the words spoken against Israel and Judah and all the nations since the time of Josiah. He therefore dictated to Baruch the scribe, who set down in writing the prophetic teaching. But though King Jehoiakim and his nobles respected the prophet himself and recognized his words as in some measure at least inspired, they did not so regard them when they were written, for the king burned the book in a brazier (Jer., ch. 36). The prophet therefore dictated the book a second time, " and many similar words were added to them " (Jer. 36:32).

Evidently, then, there was precedent for employing writing to set forth the teaching of Moses, and although the written words of later prophets were not yet regarded with special reverence, the act of King Josiah in proclaiming a national reformation on the basis of the book found in the Temple was of profound significance. He and those associated with him entertained two understandings that were subsequently to have far-reaching consequences. The first was that these were indeed the words of Moses, that he was the author of what was written. The second was that they conceived of the teaching as law rather than as prophecy. The first idea is the basis on which the rest of the books of the Pentateuch are later ascribed to Moses and called the five books of Moses; the second accounts for the fact that in the history of later Judaism, observance of the law emerged as of prime importance, more significant than prophetic teaching. The first instance of establishing a book as authentic revelation had the ultimate result of making those who followed Judaism the people of a book. Thus we see the initial stage in the appearance of Holy Scripture.

The Recognition of the Law as Scripture

The second stage occurred during the next two centuries. Thirty-five years after the reformation of Josiah, the Kingdom of Judah came to an end, and with it the Davidic dynasty. The exile effectively terminated many of the religious abuses that were condemned by Deuteronomy, but it also ended Temple worship as well. The book provided, however, a basis on which national coherence and consciousness could continue independently of Temple, palace, or capital city. The emphasis on ethical values and on the religion of the spirit put sacrifices into a secondary position. Furthermore, the fact that a written book had now become important in national faith gave added impetus to the writing of other books. Jeremiah and Ezekiel set down their messages in writing. Scribes collected and compiled the national history. An unknown prophet in exile composed the matchless chapters of consolation found in Isa., chs. 40 to 55, which have been an inspiration not only to those who were with him in Babylon but to uncounted numbers of readers ever since. Within a century after

the recognition of Deuteronomy, another code of laws was prepared, known today as the Holiness Code, comprising chapters
17 to 26 of the book of Leviticus. It is noteworthy that this code,
like the one in Deuteronomy, is also in the form of a sermon,
rather than a series of enactments. God is represented as speaking
to Moses, urging him to speak to the people, to instruct them
concerning the ways of holiness. It is in this sermon that there
appears the second half of the great commandment: "You shall
not take vengeance or bear any grudge against the sons of your
own people, but you shall love your neighbor as yourself: I am
the Lord." (Lev. 19:18.)

The history as written eventually included the entire period
from Creation to the appearance of Moses, and from Moses to the
exile and the release of Jehoiachin from imprisonment in the year
561 B.C. The national epics were set down, and found their place
in what are now Genesis and Exodus. None of this was as yet regarded as sacred, but the spirit of Deuteronomy was pervasive,
and the accounts were rewritten to bring them into line with
what was regarded as authoritative Scripture. In particular, the
interpretation of the significance of the oppressions and deliver-
ances in the days of the Judges reflects this attitude, as also the
verdicts passed upon the various rulers and other officials in the
days of the two Kingdoms.

When the exile ended, many of the people returned to Jerusalem to rebuild the city and reestablish their national life. Per-
suaded by Haggai and Zechariah, they rebuilt the Temple, and
services were resumed. The priesthood again became important.
This encouraged the codification of further legislation and the
reorganization of ritual practices, and under priestly influence
books were written incorporating genealogical and chronological
information. The religious practices of the second Temple were
embodied in the regulations and were made a part of the tradition
of the past. By the time of Ezra, just before 400 B.C., the process
of editing and compiling had reached a point where the first five
books of what is now the Bible contained both the history of

primitive and patriarchal times, and legal regulations edited in the light of contemporary practice. The ascription of the legislation to Moses was in line with what had been done two hundred years earlier, and Ezra perceived the need for standardizing a common understanding of the heritage of the past.

According to the eighth chapter of Nehemiah, a gathering of the people was held in Jerusalem in the year 444 B.C., and Ezra brought forth and read to them from what is called the book of the law of Moses. Without doubt this represents the completed Pentateuch as we now know it. A number of other persons are named as assisting on this occasion. "And they read from the book, from the law of God, clearly; and they gave the sense, so that the people understood the reading." (Neh. 8:8.) This was the beginning of preaching, the explanation of what had been read from the book. Later in the same month, the Feast of Booths was observed, and the leaders of the people covenanted for the congregation the obligation to keep the law and live in accordance with it.

By this time there were Jews in many other places throughout the world. Some had remained in Babylonia, having established themselves there, and some had emigrated to other lands about the Mediterranean. The synagogue grew up, since these widely dispersed people could hardly attend services in the Temple in Jerusalem, and the distinguishing mark of the synagogue was the reading and explanation of the law of Moses. The Pentateuch had become Scripture. It was now authoritative as a whole. It comprised all the literature existing about 400 B.C. which could be regarded as having been composed by Moses about 1200 B.C. For gradually Moses came to be looked to as the author not only of the legislation but of the national traditions as well. He was thought of as having assembled and set down the framework in which the laws are set. The entire collection was referred to as the law of Moses. The second stage in the accumulation of Scripture had been completed. Deuteronomy was now part of a larger work, all of which was held in the same esteem as had been the earlier part in the days of Josiah. Sometime later than Ezra, the Samaritan community separated from the rest of Judaism and took the Pentateuch with them as common heritage. They did not take the books of later history, for these were not yet Scripture. The descendants of the Samaritans still maintain their identity in and around the town of Nablus, a little more than thirty miles north of Jerusalem, and the Samaritan Pentateuch is one of their prized possessions. It is the only Scripture they acknowledge.

THE RECOGNITION OF THE PROPHETS AS SCRIPTURE

The designation of the five books of Moses as the Torah (Law) marks the second stage in the formation of the canon of Holy Scripture. The third stage is the recognition of the second division of the Hebrew Bible, known as the Prophets, which consists of two parts. The Former Prophets are the books of Joshua, Judges, Samuel, and Kings. The Latter Prophets are also four — Isaiah, Jeremiah, Ezekiel, and The Twelve. Much of this was in existence when the Pentateuch was formally acknowledged as authoritative, but it was still secular literature. Nevertheless, these works were treasured, for they contained material supplementary to the law, and they evidently enjoyed wide popular use.

The Former Prophets related the past glories of the nation. In accordance with the Deuteronomic theory of rewards and punishments, they indicate that men who were righteous prospered, but those who deviated from the covenant and its requirements are regarded with disfavor and receive due punishment from the Lord for their misdeeds. The Latter Prophets contained messages of judgment and looked to a better day in the future. As the sovereignty of foreign powers continued through the years, hope intensified that someday the Lord would intervene in history, right long-standing wrongs, and establish a worldwide authority in which the chosen people would receive a place of favor and pre-eminence, and Gentile nations would be judged and become subordinated to Israel. This apocalyptic hope was attached to many of the prophetic books and became part of them. Some of the lit-

erature therefore looked back to the past, tracing God's provi-
dential dealings with his people; and some looked forward to the
future, expressing the hopes and longings of a people yearning for
vindication in line with the blessings promised in the law.

It was widely believed that prophecy had ceased after the time
of Ezra. Under long years of foreign domination it seemed as if
the Lord no longer spoke to men. One of the late psalms reflects
this point of view:

> O God, why dost thou cast us off for ever?
> Why does thy anger smoke against the sheep of thy pasture?
> Remember thy congregation, which thou hast gotten of old,
> which thou hast redeemed to be the tribe of thy heritage!
>
> . . . .
>
> We do not see our signs;
> there is no longer any prophet,
> and there is none among us who knows how long.
> How long, O God, is the foe to scoff?
> Is the enemy to revile thy name for ever?
>
> (Ps. 74:1-2, 9-10.)

Diligent search was therefore made to collect the writings of
prophets of former years, and the result is found in the books
that are contained in the second section of the Hebrew Bible.
They appear to have been regarded as a kind of commentary on
the law, and sometime after the year 200 B.C. were read in the
synagogues as a part of worship on certain days.

The book of Ecclesiasticus, written about the year 180 B.C., bears
witness to the recognition of the canon of the prophets as authoritative and supplementary to the law. Chapters 44 to 49 of this
work undertake to comment on the great names of the past.

> Let us now praise famous men,
> and our fathers in their generations.
>
> (Ecclus. 44:1.)

Beginning with such patriarchs as Enoch and Noah, the list follows the order of the books in the Pentateuch, then continues through the historical works known as the Former Prophets, concluding with praise of Isaiah, Jeremiah, Ezekiel, and the Twelve Prophets. This attests to the recognition of the books of the prophetic canon as authoritative by the time this was written. The third stage in the recognition of authoritative Scripture was completed.

THE RECOGNITION OF THE WRITINGS AS SCRIPTURE

But a fourth stage was still to come. The prologue to Ecclesiasticus was written about 130 B.C. It twice mentions the sacred books, once saying that Jesus ben Sirach gave himself much " to the reading of the law and the prophets and the other books of our fathers "; and later speaking of " the law itself, the prophecies, and the rest of the books." It is clear that other works were receiving wide recognition although not regarded as Scripture. In the main part of Ecclesiasticus, which, as we have said, dates from 180 B.C., there is already an implicit recognition of additional books. Praise is given to the man who diligently seeks to learn:

> On the other hand he who devotes himself
> to the study of the law of the Most High
> will seek out the wisdom of all the ancients,
> and will be concerned with prophecies.
> (Ecclus. 39:1.)

Here law, wisdom, and prophecies represent three compilations of literature; and because of the author's special concern for wisdom, it is mentioned second, since meditations on the law had become one of the chief interests of the sages.

The Second Book of the Maccabees is variously dated by scholars from about 120 B.C. to the middle of the first Christian century. It is not regarded as an accurate historical source, but the following tradition is preserved in it: " The same things are reported in the records and in the memoirs of Nehemiah, and also that he founded a library and collected the books about the kings and prophets, and the writings of David, and letters of kings about votive offerings. In the same way Judas [Maccabeus] also collected all the books that had been lost on account of the war which had come upon us, and they are in our possession." (II Macc. 2:13-14.)

This may give some insight into the way in which other manuscripts were collected and preserved. It would appear that the collection of The Psalms was complete by the second century before Christ; it is of interest that it is divided into five books, evidently patterned after the five books of Moses. Job and The Proverbs were probably brought to their present form about the same time. But Daniel was not known to the author of Ecclesiasticus in 180 B.C., for after he has listed the great personages in the national history, he adds:

> And no man like Joseph has been born,
>   and his bones cared for.
> (Ecclus. 49:15.)

Yet Daniel, as pictured in the book of that name, was remarkably like Joseph. Carried away against his will into a foreign land, he remained true to the religion of his fathers, and rose to positions of honor and responsibility in the administration of the affairs of the land to which he had been taken. The Book of Daniel was evidently brought into its present form at a later date, as may be attested by other evidence. It may have been regarded as approaching authoritative recognition by the first century before Christ. The First Book of the Maccabees, written about 100 B.C., refers to the deliverance of Hananiah, Mishael, and Azariah from the fiery furnace, and of Daniel from the mouth of the lions (I Macc. 2:59-60).

During the century and a half following 250 B.C., the books that were treasured in Palestine in Hebrew were translated into Greek by the Jews who made Alexandria their center. They were losing their knowledge of Hebrew and wished to have the books in the language they currently used. The translation known as the Septuagint therefore gradually came into being. The only examples of it that now exist are Christian copies, so we are not really in position to know how the Alexandrian Jewish community regarded their sacred books. The existing specimens display two significant features: one is that the three canons of Law, Prophets, and Writings are disregarded, and the books were entirely rearranged and classified according to types of literature; the other is that books are included which are known to us only in Greek, and if there were Hebrew originals, these have disappeared. The Alexandrian collection probably included the books of the Apocrypha, which received recognition by the Jews of the Dispersion but were not acknowledged by the Palestinian community. The order of the books in our Bibles is derived from the rearrangement in the Greek translation.

There was still no firm recognition of Scripture beyond the Law and the Prophets by the beginning of the Christian era. Nevertheless, the psalms were so widely known and largely used that they had become an integral part of the legacy of Judaism. Since tradition ascribed them to David, it is easy to see that they were considered authoritative. Hence the New Testament writers quote them, along with the canonical Law and Prophets, to support the arguments for the Christian gospel. Because the Christians made extensive use of the Greek translation of the books of the Law and the Prophets, Judaism found it expedient to disavow the Alexandrian Septuagint, and by official action in A.D. 130, the literal translation of Aquila replaced it. But the destruction of Jerusalem in A.D. 70 made it imperative to determine what was actually considered to be authoritative Scripture, and in the year A.D. 90 the so-called Council of Jamnia, summoned by Jewish leaders, made final decision, and closed the canon of Scripture. They decreed the Law, the Prophets, and the Writings as canonical, omitting the Apocrypha, while the rest of the books that comprise our Old Testament today received recognition.

The basic principle in defining books as Holy Scripture goes back to the idea that God has spoken to men of prophetic mind. They have understood his message, and their word is his word. Beginning with the concept that the spoken word is authentic, the events we have considered lead eventually to the point where a book is decisive, not alone because it is the record of spoken words, but because in it is recognized authoritative truth which may never have been delivered in spoken form at all.

Thus it comes about that a body of writings existed, to which the Christian church could point as having authority, and by which it sought to validate its message of the gospel. The New Testament writers could point to what was written, and if they could show that the written and inspired word corresponded in some way to their own teaching, that fact would confirm the gospel. It is small wonder that the recurrent theme is seen to be: " Thus it is written; now it is fulfilled."

CHAPTER IV

Prophecy and Prediction

ONE OF THE most important contributions of modern Biblical scholarship has been the emergence of the realization that, as a rule, Biblical passages arise in particular historical settings. The historical study of the Bible has emphasized the fact that those who wrote it did so in response to actual situations. The older idea, that men of old were divinely inspired to speak words whose content was in reality a mystery to them, has been discredited. Of course they often dealt with principles and concepts whose depths they could not fathom, and they may on occasion have spoken words that would someday be seen to have significance far beyond their own realization. But we must not imagine that they spoke or wrote what was to them unintelligible.

Absence of historical perspective is what has tended to make Scripture unreal for many in our time. Many of us imagine that we are called upon to believe in a kind of religious soothsaying; that incredible visionary powers were possessed by prophets and psalmists so that they could describe in detail events that had not yet come to pass, and indeed would not occur until many generations later. Such a procedure seems to run contrary to our experience, yet the expressions so often used by New Testament writers with respect to the Old Testament Scriptures seem to demand this. Just here is where the historical approach to the Bible has recovered for us a vitality and a reality that can save us from what is, after all, an unreal view of Scripture.

The view that prophet and psalmist wrote not for their contemporaries primarily but for men who, in some later age, might discover hidden meanings in their words lays stress upon the idea of inspired prediction instead of upon realized fulfillment. Indeed, the dominant emphasis in some fringe groups and sects of Christianity is the continual attempt to make the role of the predictor more significant, as though an event could be of superior importance if it had been foretold in some miraculous way. The direction in which our investigation is taking us shows that it is, after all, not the prediction that is of value, but the result; not the supposed foretelling, but the realization of what had previously been less clearly perceived.

As an instance in point, let us look at the words of Ps. 118:22-23:

> The stone which the builders rejected
>   has become the chief cornerstone.
> This is the Lord's doing;
>   it is marvelous in our eyes.

This passage is probably one of the "testimonies" used extensively in the early church. It is quoted five times in the New Testament, in several different senses. It is found successively in Matthew, Mark, and Luke, in the book of The Acts, and in The First Letter of Peter. If it is to be regarded as a prediction, exactly what does it foretell?

The historical approach to the Bible indicates that we should first try to understand its use in the psalm. This particular psalm is one of several that were commonly used in later Old Testament times in connection with the Hebrew national festivals. Psalms 114 to 118 were called "The Great Hallel" ("The Great Praise") and were used significantly in connection with the Passover season. On the evening of his betrayal, Jesus had observed the Last Supper with his disciples, and Matthew records, "And when they had sung a hymn, they went out to the Mount of Olives" (Matt. 26:30). It is quite possible that the hymn sung on that occasion was Ps. 118, the concluding psalm of this group.

The sequence of these psalms relates to the historic faith of Israel. Psalm 114 begins with the deliverance from Egypt, recalling the great events that accompanied the beginning of the national tradition. Psalm 115 contrasts Israel's faith in the one true God with the idols of the nations about them, and ascribes to the Lord alone praise and honor. The three psalms that follow indicate the response of the people to God's gracious deliverance and their faith in the future, in which they shall continue to "recount the deeds of the Lord."

It is in this setting that we find the lines about the rejected stone which God has taken and made the cornerstone. The reference is obviously to Israel, despised among the nations, deemed of no value by her neighbors, rejected in the eyes of the world, but whom God has chosen and made his own, raising her to a position of significance in his dealings with men. The rejected stone is Israel.

The three Synoptic Gospels relate how Jesus quoted these words in conjunction with the parable of the householder who let out his vineyard to tenants, in order to illustrate his teaching about the Kingdom of God. After repeating the familiar words about the rejected stone, he said, "Therefore I tell you, the kingdom of God will be taken away from you and given to a nation producing the fruits of it" (Matt. 21:43 and parallels). The chief priests and Pharisees discerned that he was speaking about them. They had not been willing to receive and understand his message of the coming of the Kingdom. They had rejected it. But in God's providence, it was destined to become the chief cornerstone of Christ's gospel. The rejected stone is the Kingdom of God.

On the occasion when Peter and John healed the lame man in the Temple, they were summoned before the elders and scribes, in the presence of the high priest and his family, to give an account of themselves. The question was, "By what power or by what name did you do this?" Peter, with all boldness, answered: "Be it known to you all, and to all the people of Israel, that by the name of Jesus Christ of Nazareth, whom you crucified, whom

God raised from the dead, by him this man is standing before you well. This is the stone which was rejected by you builders, but which has become the head of the corner. And there is salvation in no one else." (Acts 4:8, 10-12.) According to Peter, Jesus is himself the rejected stone.

To the author of The First Letter of Peter, belief in Christ is the essence of the gospel. This is what the church preached, but which unbelievers rejected. To receive the word of the gospel is to accept that which is precious.

But for those who do not believe,

> "The very stone which the builders rejected
> has become the head of the corner,"

and

> "A stone that will make men stumble,
> a rock that will make them fall."
>
> (I Peter 2:7-8.)

The rejected stone is the gospel of Christ.

Here are three fulfillments alleged by the New Testament: successively the rejected stone is identified as the Kingdom of God, as Christ himself, and as the gospel that the church preaches about him. If we are to think primarily in terms of prediction and if we are to assume, as some have done, that the New Testament usage of an Old Testament passage determines what it meant originally, which of these three interpretations shall we choose? We must conclude, on the basis of our present understanding of Scripture, that none of these three was really the original intention. Historical study will make it plain that the original use referred to the rejected nation, Israel. The psalmist had none of the three alleged fulfillments in mind when he wrote. But, in later times, the appropriateness of the idea gives rise to the several quotations in the Gospels, The Acts, and I Peter, each with its own validity in a new situation. The emphasis, to be properly placed, must be put upon the idea of fulfillment, not on prediction. To regard the Old Testament as primarily a foretelling of the New is to present the matter in reverse.

The Meaning of Fulfillment

Several Hebrew and Greek words lie behind the English translation " fulfill." The most usual ones, in both original languages, mean simply to " fill," or " fill full." The opening words of Ps. 24 read, " The earth is the Lord's and the fulness thereof," which is then made more explicit in the parallel line that follows, " the world and those who dwell therein." The fullness of the earth consists in everything it contains. It is filled full of that which God has created. A word or phrase or idea may be capable of containing more signficance than had previously been ascribed to it. Just as a cup which is partially empty can be filled full, a saying or pronouncement may be given additional meaning.

But a further significance is seen in another group of words, both in Greek and Hebrew, related to the meaning " to complete, finish, consummate." What is only partially stated in one connection, or only begun at one time, is brought to completion in another situation. The seed which has been planted is brought to fruition by further growth. Closely related to this idea is the word, often used in the passive sense in the Greek, " to be accomplished," that is, to come to realization or actuality.

Both the Old and New Testaments also use terms which are properly translated " to raise up, to establish." This suggests the idea of support, or corroboration, resulting in verification or authentication. And lastly we may note Paul's use of still another word, when he says that the Ten Commandments, some of which he quotes, " are summed up in this sentence, ' You shall love your neighbor as yourself ' " (Rom. 13:9). To be summed up is to be brought to comprehensive and inclusive realization.

It is apparent that these terms have general as well as theological applications. Specifically, we may note at least five particular usages that are helpful in understanding what we are considering. " Fulfill " is used with the following meanings:

1. To denote the completion of a fixed time, as at the birth of a child: "When her days to be delivered were fulfilled" (Gen. 25:24; cf. Luke 2:6), or, more generally, in God's promise to Israel in connection with his covenant, "I will fulfil the number of your days" (Ex. 23:26). We may note also the preaching of John, "the time is fulfilled, and the kingdom of God is at hand" (Mark 1:15), or the reference of Jesus to the perils preceding the end of the age, "until the times of the Gentiles are fulfilled" (Luke 21:24).

2. To express the satisfaction of a request or a desire: Esther asks the king to grant her petition and fulfill her request (Esth. 5:8), the psalmist extols the faithfulness of the Lord toward his servants: "He fulfils the desire of all who fear him" (Ps. 145:19), and the writer of Proverbs notes, "A desire fulfilled is sweet to the soul" (Prov. 13:19).

3. To denote the execution of a vow: "When any one offers a sacrifice . . . to fulfil a vow" (Lev. 22:21; Num. 15:3). This use means the carrying out of what is promised.

4. To express conformity to, or obedience to, a requirement: Paul states comprehensively that "love is the fulfilling of the law" (Rom. 13:10), and again that "the whole law is fulfilled in one word, 'You shall love your neighbor as yourself'" (Gal. 5:14; so also James 2:8). Of his own baptism Jesus noted, "It is fitting for us to fulfil all righteousness" (Matt. 3:15).

5. To indicate correspondence of an event with a prior promise or announcement: this is the theological use toward which we have been directing our attention, and which is the subject of our inquiry.

It is apparent from the foregoing that according to the usage of the Bible, the word "fulfill" is employed in a wide variety of senses. It is quite impossible to assign the same significance to the word wherever it is used. In some cases it means very little more than a correspondence of phraseology; one idea reminds the author of another, and a similarity of phrase is an effective way of emphasizing a point. At other times the quotation may be by way of illustration: no actual correspondence is indicated or intended; the reference to another situation clarifies what is being said by citing a parallel or carrying the reader's imagination to another circle of events or range of ideas that gives perspective and meaning to what is presently being set forth. Still other passages consciously look for a previous presentiment or anticipation of what is now being said or done. To press all into the same mold and draw the conclusion that every "fulfillment" involves a "prediction" is quite unwarranted.

Soothsaying and Divination

I shall presently discuss my contention that the great prophets of the Old Testament understood that their first responsibility was to reach their contemporaries with the truths they proclaimed. They wanted their hearers to do something, or to believe something, or to be something. As spokesmen for God, they were primarily concerned with the divine purpose and with human response to that purpose. It is in this connection that they so often look toward the future and announce what lies ahead.

The course of the future is something that mankind has always sought to discover. Divination and soothsaying are very ancient. All the great civilizations of former times, and many modern peoples as well, have tried to uncover the mystery of what might lie ahead. A great variety of curious methods have been employed in this attempt. The oracle at Delphi was supposed by the ancient Greeks to be able to reveal the future. The strange cries and enigmatic statements of priestesses there were believed to be supernaturally inspired, and were presumably translated and interpreted by those who supervised the shrine. Sometimes the form of a supposed prediction was ambiguous enough to admit of realization in different ways, so that no matter what ensued, the oracle could be thought to have announced it. Among the peoples of the ancient world, Hebrews included, there were persons, often priests, who were called upon to interpret what were thought to be " signs," such as the form or movement of clouds, the flight of birds, involuntary human actions such as sneezing, the color, form, or movements of the liver or other organs of sacrificed animals, and other phenomena.

The basic supposition behind these and similar practices was that what men could not control was divinely determined and could be assumed to reveal divine purpose if correctly interpreted. The proverb stated,

> The lot is cast into the lap,
> but the decision is wholly from the Lord.
> (Prov. 16:33.)

Hence wide use was made in early days of the sacred lot, or arrows were shaken in a quiver, the way in which they dropped out indicating which of two or more alternatives assigned would be considered as predicted. Urim and Thummim were in use in the days of Saul and David, and while we do not know their exact nature, they could be employed to indicate alternate choice. An instance of such use is found in connection with the incident recorded of Saul's attempt to discover who had tasted food in disobedience to his prohibition of this until victory had been attained over the Philistines. The Revised Standard Version correctly includes the words, lacking in the Hebrew Bible but preserved in the Greek and Latin Bibles, " If this guilt is in me or in Jonathan my son, O Lord, God of Israel, give Urim; but if this guilt is in thy people Israel, give Thummim " (I Sam. 14:41). When Saul and Jonathan were indicated, Saul said, " ' Cast the lot between me and my son Jonathan.' And Jonathan was taken " (v. 42). The sacred lot revealed supernaturally what would otherwise have been hidden.

In early Israel, much of this sort of thing prevailed. Joseph is said to have had a cup by which he " divined," presumably by observing the forms taken by dregs of wine, or by oil poured on water. We are reminded of a modern parallel in those who aspire to fortune-telling by reading tea leaves. Gideon sought a sign in a dry fleece on wet ground, or a wet fleece on dry ground (Judg. 6:36 ff.). When David was fighting the Philistines, he looked for an omen in "the sound of marching in the tops of the balsam trees," portraying the marching of the Lord to give him victory over the enemy (II Sam. 5:24). Saul resorted to necromancy in consulting the medium at Endor, asking her to divine the future by bringing up Samuel from the dead. The reason given for this decision was that "when Saul inquired of the Lord, the Lord did not answer him, either by dreams, or by Urim, or by prophets" (I Sam. 28:6). It is said that King Ahaz, at a later time, set aside a special bronze altar "to inquire by" (II Kings 16:15).

Such practices were indulged in by most of the peoples of antiquity. Ezekiel figuratively pictures the king of Babylon standing at the parting of the way to use divination. "He shakes the arrows, he consults the teraphim, he looks at the liver. Into his right hand comes the lot for Jerusalem." (Ezek. 21:21-22.) But as a result of the teaching of the prophets, these activities came to be frowned upon as pagan. Isaiah has this to say of necromancy: "When they say to you, ' Consult the mediums and the wizards who chirp and mutter,' should not a people consult their God? Should they consult the dead on behalf of the living?" (Isa. 8:19). The prophetic author of Deuteronomy expressly forbids these pagan practices: "There shall not be found among you any one who burns his son or his daughter as an offering, any one who practices divination, a soothsayer, or an augur, or a sorcerer, or a charmer, or a medium, or a wizard, or a necromancer. For whoever does these things is an abomination to the Lord" (Deut. 18:10-12). Hosea pours scorn upon divination by means of a staff:

> My people inquire of a thing of wood,
>   and their staff gives them oracles.
> For a spirit of harlotry has led them astray,
>   and they have left their God to play the harlot.
>   (Hos. 4:12.)

It is clear that the more mature position resulting from the in-spiration of the prophets discountenances divination. This kind of attempt to discern the future is not compatible with prophetic un-derstanding of the ways of God. It belongs to more primitive at-tempts to pry open the future, and is out of keeping with true knowledge of the will of God.

CAN A PROPHET MAKE A MISTAKE?

Beginning in the eighth century before Christ, the prophets found themselves in frequent conflict with contemporary profes-sional prophets who relied heavily on dreams, omens, and other forms of divination. In Jeremiah's time such prophets said, in effect, "You shall not see the sword, nor shall you have famine, but I will give you assured peace in this place" (Jer. 14:13). Jere-miah denounced them, indicating that the Lord had said: "I did not send them, nor did I command them or speak to them. They are prophesying to you a lying vision, worthless divination, and the deceit of their own minds" (v. 14). Jeremiah also warned: "Do not listen to your prophets, your diviners, your dreamers, your soothsayers, or your sorcerers, who are saying to you, 'You shall not serve the king of Babylon.' For it is a lie which they are prophesying to you" (Jer. 27:9-10).

Zechariah 10:2 declares:

> For the teraphim utter nonsense,
>   and the diviners see lies;
> the dreamers tell false dreams,
>   and give empty consolation.
> Therefore the people wander like sheep;
>   they are afflicted for want of a shepherd.

Micah observed that easy messages of false security were spoken because these were what the nation wanted to hear.

> Its heads give judgment for a bribe,
>   its priests teach for hire,

> its prophets divine for money;
> yet they lean upon the Lord and say,
>   "Is not the Lord in the midst of us?
> No evil shall come upon us."
>
>   (Micah 3:11.)

By contrast, the true prophet was constrained to speak an unwelcome message because of divine compulsion.

> But as for me, I am filled with power,
>   with the Spirit of the Lord,
>   and with justice and might,
> to declare to Jacob his transgression
>   and to Israel his sin.
>
>   (Micah 3:8.)

The distinction between true and false prophets is first seen in the case of Micaiah, who announced to Ahab prior to his proposed attack on Ramoth-gilead that his campaign would fail. This was directly in opposition to the word of about four hundred other prophets who encouraged the king to proceed, and who promised victory. Micaiah did not deny inspiration to the four hundred, but stated, curiously enough, that the Lord himself had sent forth a lying spirit, to entice Ahab, and that this spirit had been put into the mouths of these men (I Kings 22:5-23). This interpretation saved the idea of prophetic inspiration at the expense of making the Lord himself responsible for falsehood. A different approach is made in Deuteronomy: "When a prophet speaks in the name of the Lord, if the word does not come to pass or come true, that is a word which the Lord has not spoken; the prophet has spoken it presumptuously, you need not be afraid of him." (Deut. 18:22.) Thus, the verification of a prediction by subsequent events is made the criterion of truth or falsity. This may be satisfactory as far as it goes, but is quite impractical to apply as a contemporary means of judgment. It could be used only in retrospect. Who would know at the time a prophecy was made how to judge it?

As a matter of fact, Deuteronomy also recognizes that fulfillment of a prediction may not be a valid test after all. "If a prophet arises among you, or a dreamer of dreams, and gives you a sign or a wonder, and the sign or wonder which he tells you comes to pass, and if he says, 'Let us go after other gods,' which you have not known, 'and let us serve them,' you shall not listen to the words of that prophet or to that dreamer of dreams; for the Lord your God is testing you." (Deut. 13:1-3.)

This latter approach is also taken by Jeremiah in his lengthy discussion of the false prophets (Jer. 23:9-40). For him the criterion is not realization or nonrealization of prediction, but rather, an evaluation of the content of the message and the character of the person delivering it. An unwelcome message of distress and doom is more probably true than one that lulls into inaction with a sense that all is well. Moreover, says Jeremiah, the false prophets are men of immoral lives, thinking of their own welfare and desires, unconcerned with the social and religious evils that surround them. They are not zealous to turn men from unrighteous ways. To those who stubbornly follow the desires of their own hearts they say, "No evil shall come upon you." The real fact is that they have no message from the Lord. They have not stood in his council; they give no evidence of understanding the demands of an ethical God. Their message is not even their own: "Behold, I am against the prophets, says the Lord, who steal my words from one another." Moreover,

> They have healed the wound of my people lightly,
>   saying "Peace, peace,"
>   when there is no peace.

(Jer. 8:11.)

The word "peace" here refers not only to international harmony but generally to health and well-being. These men gloss over obvious sins with the easy phrase "All is well, all is well," when to Jeremiah it is perfectly clear that all is not well.

In contrast to such unreliable leadership, according to Jeremiah, the true prophet has an overwhelming sense of direct contact with the will of the Lord and of being dominated by him. He is impelled to speak in ways often unwelcome to his hearers. Much as he might like to echo the pleasant assurances of those who oppose him, he cannot do so, because of a will confronting him that is stronger than his desire. This will is like an inward fire, clarifying his spiritual perception so that he discerns a consistent moral purpose in God's world, and is imbued with a sense of mission to point out that sin and inconstancy can bring about only one result, and that judgment and retribution lie in store for those who will not respond to the divine word.

Precision in Prediction

Some notable instances occur, within the prophetical books, of specific predictions that found fulfillment in remarkable fashion. The first of the so-called "writing prophets" was Amos, who preached at Bethel about the middle of the eighth century before Christ. His book is a stern denunciation of carelessness and corruption prevailing in an age of prosperity. The reign of Jeroboam II was characterized by peace and apparent security, by accumulated wealth in the hands of some and poverty on the part of others, by oppression of the poor, by dishonesty in trading, by bribery and injustice on the part of those in authority, and by prevalent immorality. Yet the people were zealous in attendance at the solemn assemblies, in offering sacrifices, in keeping their feasts, and in payment of their religious tithes. Justice and mercy were seemingly no part of prevailing religion. In his scathing denunciation of these conditions, Amos predicted in no uncertain terms that God's punishment would fall, the land would be shaken from end to end, and the people would go into captivity at the hands of invading armies. Interestingly enough, within two years there occurred one of the most memorable earthquakes of Biblical times, and hardly a generation had passed before the Assyrian armies came, and with the fall of Samaria, brought the northern kingdom of Israel to its end. Probably we should note that the earthquake was not necessarily the realization of the prediction, for the "shaking" could result from warfare, but certainly the invasion of the enemy brought about the kind of doom that Amos had pronounced. His words were remarkably vindicated.

Another instance of realization of a prediction is seen in the way in which Isaiah tried to reassure Ahaz, king of Judah, during the threat of attack upon Jerusalem by the combined forces of Syria and Israel in 735-734 B.C. This was the occasion of the "Immanuel" prophecy, which we have mentioned elsewhere.

The point is, however, that Isaiah's advice was "take heed, be quiet, do not fear," for before a child, whose birth was said to be imminent, could be old enough to distinguish good and evil, the peril from the northern alliance would have disappeared (Isa. 7:16). Moreover, before another infant could be old enough to say, "my father" or "my mother," the lands of Syria and Israel would be despoiled by the Assyrians (Isa. 8:4). This is exactly what happened. The prediction was verified by events that followed.

Later, when Sennacherib invaded Judah, Isaiah assured King Hezekiah that "he shall not come into this city, or shoot an arrow there, or come before it with a shield, or cast up a siege mound against it. . . . He shall not come into this city, says the Lord. For I will defend this city to save it" (Isa. 37:33-35). History records that for some reason Sennacherib did not attempt to take Jerusalem, that, though he devastated other parts of the Palestinian coastland, he broke off his campaign and returned to Nineveh. Archaeology has recovered his own annals of this expedition, and though he claims to have "shut up Hezekiah like a caged bird" in his capital city, it is clear that Jerusalem did not capitulate to him. The prediction of Isaiah thus found realization in a remarkable way.

Once more, we note the occasion when Jeremiah opposed the false prophet Hananiah, denouncing him for having made the people trust in a lie, and adding, "This very year you shall die, because you have uttered rebellion against the Lord." The following verse adds that Hananiah died in the same year, in the seventh month (Jer. 28:16-17). Conversely, when Hezekiah was sick and at the point of death, Isaiah gave as the word of the Lord that he should set his house in order, for he was not to recover, but die. After Hezekiah showed indications of contrition, the prophet reversed his message and said that the Lord had heard his prayer, that the span of his life would be increased by another fifteen years. Deliverance from Sennacherib was also promised (Isa. 38:1-6). Hezekiah did recover from his illness, and as we have seen, the city was delivered.

Somewhat different in character is the prediction of Ahijah that the kingdom of Solomon would be divided. Solomon's splendid building projects were costly and required heavy taxation. This brought about increasing resentment, especially on the part of the northern tribes, who were thus called upon to contribute to the glory of Jerusalem. An active member of the dissenting faction was Jeroboam, who may be described in modern terminology as a young labor leader. The prophet Ahijah went out to talk with him in the open country, wearing a new cloak. He took hold of the garment, tore it into twelve pieces, gave ten of them to Jeroboam, and said, "Take for yourself ten pieces; for thus says the Lord, the God of Israel, 'Behold, I am about to tear the kingdom from the hand of Solomon, and will give you ten tribes'" (I Kings 11:29-31). Jeroboam fled to Egypt to escape the wrath of Solomon and remained there until Solomon's death. But with the accession of Rehoboam, Solomon's son, he returned and resumed leadership of the opposition, demanding that the new king lighten the oppressive yoke of taxation and conscripted labor. Rehoboam refused, and the writer of the First Book of Kings interprets, "It was a turn of affairs brought about by the Lord that he might fulfil his word, which the Lord spoke by Ahijah the Shilonite to Jeroboam" (I Kings 12:15). Rebellion followed almost immediately, and Jeroboam became king over the ten northern tribes.

In this instructive example, we find a prediction which was fulfilled, but we certainly do not assume that the forecast was made apart from the existing situation. In fact, by foretelling what would happen, the prophet was releasing the motivating power that brought about its fulfillment. Ahijah was no passive on-looker; he was an active, dynamic participant in the whole chain of events. In a sense, the foretelling of the revolt was one means of making it come to pass.

In the instances that have just been cited we observe foretelling of doom or of deliverance which is to befall the person to whom the prediction is being made. In each case, the future is directly connected with the present and is an outcome and consequence of the circumstances to which the prophet is directing attention. The religious, spiritual, and moral elements in the situation are of first importance. The future is in a real sense part of the cur-rent scene, and grows out of it. There is a vital connection be-tween the two. This is quite different from a long-range predic-tion that presupposes that history is predestined and fatalistically conceived, and that it must inevitably unfold along the lines de-scribed, no matter what happens. The prophets never thought of history as unalterably predetermined. There was always a sense in which present and future were connected.

CONDITIONAL PREDICTIONS

This leads us to note that prophetic predictions were in a sense conditional. Jeremiah makes this explicit in his well-known ob-servations concerning the potter, who can shape or reshape a ves-sel according to his wishes. He immediately compares this free-dom with the Lord's treatment of his people: "If at any time I declare concerning a nation or a kingdom, that I will pluck up and break down and destroy it, and if that nation, concerning which I have spoken, turns from its evil, I will repent of the evil that I intended to do to it. And if at any time I declare concern-ing a nation or a kingdom that I will build and plant it, and if it does evil in my sight, not listening to my voice, then I will re-pent of the good which I had intended to do to it." (Jer. 18:7-10.)

Jeremiah then pronounces evil upon Judah, and immediately follows with an appeal for amendment of the ways and doings of the people. It is evident that the purpose of prediction was not simply to foretell a future event without reference to present conditions, but to induce a response to the prophetic word in conformity with the implications of the prediction.

Instances may be cited from the books of Kings concerning particular predictions attributed to Elijah, Elisha, and others, both concerning particular persons and concerning the people as a whole. Since these books were written long after the events narrated, as an interpretation as well as an account of what took place in Israel's past, it is difficult for us to know to what extent the form of words in which the predictions are stated may be colored by subsequent developments. In retrospect, the forecast might be in part fashioned according to the outcome. Scholars are convinced that the name of Josiah has thus been inserted into the prophecy of an unnamed prophet who at Bethel announced doom upon the house of Jeroboam and foretold destruction of the altar he considered to be spurious (I Kings 13:2), an outcome which is related to have taken place as part of Josiah's reformation three centuries later (II Kings 23:15-16).

An early designation for a prophet was the term " seer." It was applied to one who observes and discerns clearly. In its origin, it probably called attention to attempts to discover what lay ahead. Forms of divination were no doubt employed, for this was one way of "inquiring of the Lord." Samuel was called both seer and prophet. Saul was urged by his servant to consult Samuel concerning the lost animals they were searching for, because " he is a man that is held in honor; all that he says comes true . . . ; perhaps he can tell us about the journey on which we have set out " (I Sam. 9:6). Included in the account is an explanatory statement by the historian: "Formerly in Israel, when a man went to inquire of God, he said, ' Come, let us go to the seer '; for he who is now called a prophet was formerly called a seer." (I Sam. 9:9.)

Thus it is clear that a forecast of coming events was a legitimate part of prophecy, and the instances that we have been noting demonstrate that on many occasions the insights were vindicated by the outcome. Predictions were fulfilled. But this is not universally true in the Bible. While many forecasts were historically realized, others were not. Let us examine some of these.

Unfulfilled Predictions

A careful reading of the Old Testament will make it plain that numerous predictions were not fulfilled. These are a part of the whole problem, and must also be taken into account. Even the canonical prophets made forecasts that did not come to pass, and in the very nature of the case, never can come to pass.

One of these is found in Ezekiel's oracle against Tyre. The passage says: "For thus says the Lord God: Behold, I will bring upon Tyre from the north Nebuchadrezzar king of Babylon, king of kings, with horses and chariots, and with horsemen and a host of many soldiers. . . . Your walls will shake at the noise of the horsemen and wagons and chariots, when he enters your gates as one enters a city which has been breached. With the hoofs of his horses he will trample all your streets; he will slay your people with the sword; and your mighty pillars will fall to the ground. . . . I will make you a bare rock; you shall be a place for the spreading of nets; you shall never be rebuilt; for I the Lord have spoken." (Ezek. 26:7-14.)

But Nebuchadrezzar did not take Tyre. His siege failed. Ezekiel himself realized that this was the case, and therefore made a new prediction at a later date, in which he admitted that "Nebuchadrezzar king of Babylon made his army labor hard against Tyre; every head was made bald and every shoulder was rubbed bare; yet neither he nor his army got anything from Tyre to pay for the labor that he had performed against it. Therefore thus says the Lord God: Behold, I will give the land of Egypt to Nebuchadrezzar king of Babylon; and he shall carry off its wealth and despoil it and plunder it; and it shall be the wages for his army." (Ezek. 29:18-19.)

As a matter of sober historical record, we may add that the siege of Tyre lasted for about thirteen years, from 585 to 572 B.C., but was unsuccessful. Part of Tyre was on an island, half a mile offshore, now joined by a sand spit to the mainland. The Tyrians were able to hold off the enemy, and eventually came to terms with Nebuchadrezzar. But the city was not conquered or destroyed, "never to be rebuilt," as Ezekiel had previously predicted. Hence, the prophet held that Egypt should be the Babylonian's reward. He shared this expectation with Jeremiah, who was taken by his compatriots to Egypt against his will after the destruction of Jerusalem and the murder of Gedaliah. Jeremiah announced at Tahpanhes: "Thus says the Lord of hosts, the God of Israel: Behold, I will send and take Nebuchadrezzar the king of Babylon, my servant. . . . He shall come and smite the land of Egypt. . . . He shall kindle a fire in the temples of the gods of Egypt; and he shall burn them and carry them away captive. . . . He shall break the obelisks of Heliopolis which is in the land of Egypt; and the temples of the gods of Egypt he shall burn with fire." (Jer. 43:10-13.)

But these predictions also did not come to pass. A very fragmentary text in the British Museum seems to indicate that after the siege of Tyre was ended, Nebuchadrezzar marched against Egypt to engage in battle with Ahmose II. We do not know the outcome. It seems improbable that more than a border skirmish took place, and in any case it is certain that Nebuchadrezzar did not conquer the land, for Ahmose continued through a long and prosperous reign. Egypt maintained its independence until conquered by Cambyses, when the Persian empire claimed it. It is quite unlikely that Nebuchadrezzar accomplished the kind of destruction envisioned by Jeremiah. As to the obelisks of Heliopolis, one of the earliest, set up in the twelfth dynasty by Sesostris I, is still in place. Another, erected by Thutmose III in the fifteenth century B.C., was removed by Constantine to Rome, where it was set up in the Circus Maximus, and in 1552 reerected near the basilica of St. John Lateran, where it stands today. Two others, also set up by Thutmose III, were taken by Caesar Augustus about 14 B.C. to adorn his new constructions in Alexandria, and in 1878–1880 were given to Britain and the United States. One of them now stands on the Thames Embankment in London, and the other is in Central Park, New York; they are popularly known as "Cleopatra's Needles." Thus we observe that the details of the prediction of Jeremiah did not find realization. His purpose in making the announcement was to impress upon his fellow countrymen that fleeing to Egypt would not remove them from the sphere of Nebuchadrezzar's influence, as they so fondly hoped.

Two more instances of prediction that we may consider are found in the preaching of Micah. As punishment for the transgressions of the people, he announces the impending destruction of Samaria, whose stones will be poured down into the valley (Micah 1:6), and of Jerusalem:

> Therefore because of you
>   Zion shall be plowed as a field;
> Jerusalem shall become a heap of ruins,
>   and the mountain of the house a wooded height.
>   (Micah 3:12.)

Within the lifetime of the prophet his prediction about Samaria found realization in its destruction by the Assyrians, but Jerusalem was spared. Only some generations later did Zion fall, and one cannot assert with any certainty that the Temple area ever became particularly wooded. More than a century after Micah, it is recorded that the elders, who had been alerted to the words of doom spoken by Jeremiah, took note of Micah's previous prediction, and observed that it had not been fulfilled because Hezekiah feared the Lord and entreated his favor, so that the Lord repented of the evil which had been pronounced against the city. Fulfillment therefore did not take place as anticipated, although we note an eventual destruction under other circumstances.

Two Kinds of Predictive Prophecy

Predictive passages in the prophets appear to fall into two general classes. On the one hand are those which look to the more immediate future, whose outcome is in some considerable measure an outgrowth of the present, and whose realization is related to the current situation and to the response of the prophet's hearers to his message. On the other hand are predictions that look to a consummation " at the end of the days." These are eschatological, representing an ultimate or final conclusion toward which the word of the prophet points. They look forward to the establishment of the Lord's universal purpose, the correspondence of the things of this world to the ideals that ought to be, and to the ultimate renewal of all things according to a grand design for man and the world.

In the nature of the case, it is the first group, those related to the more immediate future, of which we are more nearly able to estimate fulfillment or nonfulfillment in history. A wide variety of prophetic pronouncements comprise this category. They range all the way from the individual and personal to the national and general. Jeremiah gave oracles concerning several of the kings of Judah in his time. Of Jehoiakim he predicted that his death would not be lamented and that he would remain unburied, " dragged and cast forth beyond the gates of Jerusalem " (Jer. 22:19). We do not have sufficient evidence to be able to judge to what extent this prediction may have been fulfilled. II Kings 24:6 records that " Jehoiakim slept with his fathers," which ordinarily would indicate burial in a tomb according to custom; but it may be conjectured that he lost his life by assassination at the hands of some who disagreed with his foreign policy, or that after he was buried his tomb was in some way dishonored. We simply do not have enough data to decide.

Jehoiakim was succeeded by his son Jehoiachin, who came to the throne at the age of eighteen, reigned three months, and was taken into exile in Babylon. Concerning him, Jeremiah said,

> Write this man down as childless,
>   a man who shall not succeed in his days;
> for none of his offspring shall succeed
>   in sitting on the throne of David,
>   and ruling again in Judah.
>
> > (Jer. 22:30.)

Jehoiachin lived in exile for many years, apparently with a good deal of liberty, then, being imprisoned at a later time, was eventually freed by Evil-merodach (a Hebrew rendering of Awel-Marduk; not a value judgment), king of Babylon, and given a place of preeminence among other kings who were also exiled. " He dined regularly at the king's table; and for his allowance, a regular allowance was given him by the king, every day a portion, as long as he lived." (II Kings 25:29-30.) But he did not die childless. I Chronicles 3:17-18 records the names of his seven sons; his grandson was Zerubbabel, prominent in the time of the return from exile, and apparently looked to by Haggai and Zechariah as associated with the reestablishment of Judah's independence, almost in messianic fashion (Zech. 4:6-14; 6:10-13). Matthew includes the name of Jehoiachin in the genealogy of Jesus, naming him as the father of Shealtiel and the grandfather of Zerubbabel (Matt. 1:12).

Among other personal oracles may be cited one pronounced by Amos upon Amaziah, the priest of Bethel. Amaziah had reported Amos as having predicted doom for Jeroboam II, the king, saying,

> Jeroboam shall die by the sword,
>   and Israel must go into exile
>   away from his land.
>
> > (Amos 7:11.)

We do not know that Jeroboam died by the sword. It seems unlikely, for the historical books record that during his long reign of forty-one years he conducted successful military campaigns, in

which " he restored the border of Israel from the entrance of
Hamath as far as the Sea of the Arabah," and that the Lord
" saved them [his people] by the hand of Jeroboam," after which
he " slept with his fathers, the kings of Israel." (II Kings 14:25-
29.) But Amos went on also to denounce Amaziah for attempting
to silence him, predicting that his family would fall by the sword,
and that he himself would die in exile in a foreign land. This
indicates that the prophet saw him as participating in the down-
fall that was portrayed for the nation.

Jeremiah's prediction concerning Pashhur the priest, who had
punished him for his preaching, indicated that Pashhur and his
house would participate in the exile in Babylon (Jer. 20:1-6).
Moreover, we note Isaiah's denunciation of Shebna, an important
functionary who was "over the household," predicting that he
would be thrust from his office and cast down from his station
(Isa. 22:15-19). Assuming that this is the same Shebna mentioned in a later chapter, he is there designated as "secretary,"
among those civilians who were summoned to consult with the
Babylonian military leaders over prospective terms of capitula-
tion. If he was demoted from the office of palace governor to a
position as state secretary, he was still in an office of great responsibility. The prophet's original polemic against him probably reflected a feeling that he had thought too much of his own status
and had given insufficient time to affairs of state.

Further oracles found in the books of the prophets concern the
people and nation. We have already given consideration to a number of these, finding some fulfilled and others failing of realization in subsequent events. In some instances, parts of the predictions received verification, others did not. It would appear that
sometimes a prophet, having made a general forecast, filled in the
details for the sake of vividness and amplification, perhaps without expecting these further elements actually to occur. Perhaps he
felt that realization in terms of principle would be sufficient. Or,
perhaps he considered the prediction to be more a signpost for the
present, pointing out moral and religious principles, rather than

a blueprint of what should afterward happen. As we have already indicated, the prophetic view of history was dynamic rather than static, it was partly conditional rather than predetermined, it never represented future history to be like a motion picture film, where the entire plot is already photographed and edited, so that the present represents the frame passing the lens at a particular moment, and the future will inevitably unroll in like fashion at a predetermined time. This is not the nature of Hebrew prophecy.

Predictions Related to the End of the Age

A second great class of prophetic predictions comprises those which relate to a final consummation for which the prophet hoped, and which he anticipated should one day be realized. A great many instances of this kind of prophecy occur. Most of them have not yet come to pass historically. We refer to such pictures of the future as the wolf dwelling with the lamb, and the lion eating straw like the ox (Isa. 11:6-9), or the wealth of Egypt and Ethiopia being brought to Israel by nations in chains (Isa. 45:14), or all the nations of the earth making pilgrimage year after year to keep the Feast of Booths in Jerusalem (Zech. 14:16-18). No doubt these and similar passages are in great measure symbolic. They belong to the large group of sayings which look forward to a day when perils and disappointments of life will be done away, when peace and prosperity will prevail, and when

. . . the earth shall be full of the knowledge of the Lord
   as the waters cover the sea.

(Isa. 11:9; Hab. 2:14.)

A large number of Old Testament forecasts selected by New Testament writers are drawn from this second group, prophecies of the end of the age. The conviction of the church is that in Christ a new dispensation has begun, and while realization in full is deferred, nevertheless the process has been initiated that leads to this kind of goal. The Christian position is that the Kingdom of God is here, and with it the beginning of the end of the age, toward which prophecy looked. The Kingdom has not come in its completeness, but its presence is asserted; it, too, needs to come in its fullness in the future, but its existence in the present is confidently affirmed. It is seen as both here and there, both now and then, both present and yet to come. And the universal kingdom is directly related to the hopes for the last days as proclaimed by the seers of old.

Old Testament delineations of the end of the age are varied in content, symbolism, and description, but there are certain consistent features that may be discerned. Though the imagery is usually specific, these formulations must be considered to be representative or typical rather than actual. The basic elements comprise a combination of two features, *judgment* and *salvation*. These two elements are applied not so much to individual persons as to Israel and the other nations of the world. Judgment is almost always linked to salvation, and precedes it; judgment is not, as a rule, an end in itself.

Old Testament designations for the end of the age are usually such as " The Day of the Lord," " Behold, days are coming," " in that day," " in those days," and the like. They are earlier counterparts of the New Testament idea of a Day of Judgment. The concept is set forth in many of the prophetic books — notably in Amos, Joel, Zephaniah, Zechariah, and throughout The Book of Isaiah. The Day of the Lord is darkness, not light, for the people. It is portrayed as preceded by, or including, catastrophes of national or cosmic character. Visitations are of two general types — those due to natural causes and those due to human causes. Among the first we note such disasters as flood, earthquake, pestilence, famine, and even world conflagration, together with heavenly portents, such as eclipse, the sun and moon being darkened, or " turned into blood," or the stars being blotted out. Catastrophes attributable to human agency are usually in the form of war and conflict, with the usual resulting devastation emphasized to a high degree, or in terms of the breakdown of law and order, resulting in prevailing anarchy and strife. What is represented is the overthrow of stable human relationships and the substitution of generally chaotic conditions.

These visitations are represented either as preceding God's judgment, or as part of it. The imperfections and transgressions of men reap the rewards they have earned. The judgment is first on Israel; but more than that, it is on the nations in general, since God is Lord of all of his creation. Zephaniah characterizes this as

> A day of wrath . . . ,
>   a day of distress and anguish,
> a day of ruin and devastation,
>   a day of darkness and gloom,
> a day of clouds and thick darkness.
> > (Zeph. 1:15.)

Jerusalem is laid waste and plundered, the stroke falling on officials and kings' sons as well as on traders and common folk.

> Neither their silver nor their gold
>   shall be able to deliver them
> on the day of the wrath of the Lord.
> > (Zeph. 1:18.)

In the representation of Joel, all the peoples are gathered together to a place called "the valley of Jehoshaphat" (i.e., The Lord has judged). This is not to be thought of as a particular named place, though in modern times the name has been attached to the Kidron Valley east of Jerusalem. It is rather a symbolic location. Here the Lord enters into judgment with the nations, "on account of my . . . heritage Israel, because they have scattered them among the nations, and have divided up my land" (Joel 3:2). Figures are sometimes drawn from the harvest: the nations are subject to the sickle, the wine press is full, ready for treading, and "the vats overflow, for their wickedness is great" (Joel 3:13). Such representations as these may be paralleled from others of the prophets, in great variety.

But judgment leads to salvation. Frequently it is national deliverance, with Israel and Judah restored to peace and prosperity, and the Gentile nations rendered powerless, as, for example,

Egypt shall become a desolation
  and Edom a desolate wilderness,
for the violence done to the people of Judah,
  because they have shed innocent blood in their land.
But Judah shall be inhabited for ever,
  and Jerusalem to all generations.

(Joel 3:19-20.)

In Zephaniah, destruction is visited upon Moab and Ammon, upon Assyria and Ethiopia (Zeph. 2:8-15). Each of the Major Prophets contains a series of chapters devoted to woes against surrounding nations, though the judgments indicated are not in every case specifically connected with the Day of the Lord (Isa., chs. 13 to 22; Jer., chs. 46 to 51; Ezek., chs. 25 to 32). Such oracles are characteristic of the prophetic books.

It is understandable how the judgment and punishment of God would be expected to fall upon those peoples who had brought about an end of Judah's independence, and among whom Israel was dispersed. Nevertheless, intermarriage with members of these other peoples took place, though patriots after the return from exile were of the opinion that this should cease. It seemed to them that Israel thus risked losing her national identity as well as her independence. Nehemiah prohibited mixed marriages for the future (Neh. 13:23-31), while Ezra proclaimed strict observance of the law of Moses, in order to distinguish his people from the Gentiles. He, too, banned mixed marriages, but went farther than Nehemiah in that he compelled the breaking up of all marriages which had hitherto been contracted with " foreign women from the peoples of the lands " (Ezra 10:2-4). This policy of separation increased the spirit of exclusiveness among the Jews as well as hostility toward the other nations.

Against this background, we may observe the harsh judgments pronounced against foreign peoples in the Old Testament books, and the forecast of punishment upon them. But we should note that there were also voices raised for an opposite point of view.

It may be that the author of The Book of Ruth, who portrays Ruth as a person of character and honor, wished to protest against blind nationalism by calling attention to this woman of Moab who was the great-grandmother of David. Similarly, The Book of Jonah is a great proclamation that the God of Israel is also the God of Nineveh, one who calls that city to repentance, who is ready to forgive its people, and whose concern is not alone for Israel but for her enemy as well. And let us not omit the reference in The Book of Isaiah to God's chosen people: "In that day there will be a highway from Egypt to Assyria, and the Assyrian will come into Egypt, and the Egyptian into Assyria, and the Egyptians will worship with the Assyrians. In that day Israel will be the third with Egypt and Assyria, a blessing in the midst of the earth, whom the Lord of hosts has blessed, saying, 'Blessed be Egypt my people, and Assyria the work of my hands, and Israel my heritage.'" (Isa. 19:23-25.)

Those who consider the Old Testament to be purely nationalistic in its teaching, making no place for any except the descendants of Jacob, have failed to see the universal emphasis that comes out strikingly in some of its greatest passages. A beginning is made in the traditional promise to Abraham, in which he is to become the ancestor of a great nation, "and by you all the families of the earth shall bless themselves" (Gen. 12:3). This is a recurrent theme throughout the book of Genesis (see chs. 18:18; 22:18; 26:4; 28:14), and is paralleled in Solomon's prayer of dedication of the Temple: "When a foreigner . . . comes and prays toward this house, hear thou in heaven thy dwelling place, and do according to all for which the foreigner calls to thee; in order that all the peoples of the earth may know thy name and fear thee." (I Kings 8:41-43.) Only so does the Temple find its full realization:

> . . . my house shall be called a house of prayer
> for all peoples.
>
> (Isa. 56:7.)

The Servant of the Lord has a mission

> . . . as a light to the nations,
>> that my salvation may reach to the end of the earth.
>>> (Isa. 49:6.)

This same prophet exclaims,

>> Turn to me and be saved,
>>> all the ends of the earth!
>> For I am God, and there is no other.
>>> (Isa. 45:22.)

Although Ps. 72 calls for God's victorious blessing upon the King in Zion, before whom all kings fall down, it concludes,

>> May his name endure for ever,
>>> . . . .
>> May men bless themselves by him,
>>> all nations call him blessed!
>>>> (Ps. 72:17.)

And another psalm prays that God will be universally known and worshiped:

>> that thy way may be known upon earth,
>>> thy saving power among all nations.
>> Let the peoples praise thee, O God;
>>> let all the peoples praise thee!
>> Let the nations be glad and sing for joy,
>>> for thou dost judge the peoples with equity
>>> and guide the nations upon earth.
>>>> (Ps. 67:2-4.)

It is true that with the dispersion of Israel in foreign lands, this motif became fainter and fainter; yet its persistence is seen in the résumé of Israel's history as given by the son of Sirach in the Apocrypha, as late as the second century B.C., where this writer notes that Abraham's faith resulted in God's assurance "that the nations would be blessed through his posterity " (Ecclus. 44:21). Even Zechariah, for all his nationalism, makes a place for the Gentiles in God's purpose: " And many nations shall join themselves to the Lord in that day, and shall be my people " (Zech. 2:11), and again, " Many peoples and strong nations shall come to seek the Lord of hosts in Jerusalem, and to entreat the favor of the Lord " (Zech. 8:22).

In the great portrayal of the coming of universal peace " in the latter days," many peoples are pictured as streaming to Zion to be taught by the Lord, and

> He shall judge between the nations,
>   and shall decide for many peoples;
> and they shall beat their swords into plowshares,
>   and their spears into pruning hooks;
> nation shall not lift up sword against nation,
>   neither shall they learn war any more.
>   (Isa. 2:4; Micah 4:3.)

In this passage, perhaps one of the best known and certainly one of the greatest delineations of the goal toward which human society must move, it is clear that any preeminence of Israel really is the preeminence of the God of Israel, who is also the God of all nations as well. The nationalism of many prophetic expressions must therefore be qualified and tempered by the strain of universalism that also runs through the Old Testament. It belongs to the realm of eschatology, that is, the final goal of history, and describes the ultimate conditions that prophetic insight confidently announces will someday prevail. It is small wonder, therefore, that the New Testament repeatedly picks up this theme. It represents Jesus as " a light for revelation to the Gentiles " (Luke 2:32). The Great Commission in Matthew has as its goal to " make disciples of all nations, baptizing them in the name of the Father and of the Son and of the Holy Spirit, teaching them to observe all that I have commanded you " (Matt. 28:19-20); and in Acts 1:8 the risen Lord commissions his disciples to " be my witnesses in Jerusalem and in all Judea and Samaria and to the end of the earth."

Other elements are comprised in the varied forecasts of the prophets describing the end of the age. One of these is the hope of resurrection from the dead. It was first conceived as the rebirth of a dead nation, as in Ezekiel's vision of the valley of dry bones that come to life through the breathing in of the Spirit of God (Ezek. 37:1-14). It is perhaps reflected in a late apocalyptic section inserted in The Book of Isaiah,

> Thy dead shall live, their bodies shall rise.
> O dwellers in the dust, awake and sing for joy!
> (Isa. 26:19.)

The hope is clearly for individuals in Dan. 12:2-3: " And many of those who sleep in the dust of the earth shall awake, some to everlasting life, and some to shame and everlasting contempt. And those who are wise shall shine like the brightness of the firmament; and those who turn many to righteousness, like the stars for ever and ever."

National resurrection is expressed in a return of the people from the lands of the dispersion, restoration of national identity, and the reestablishment of the throne of David through the Messianic king. National renewal is forecast, but also spiritual renewal as well. Return to the homeland is pictured as accompanied by cleansing from stains of unfaithfulness and sin, and by purification of national spirit: " I will sprinkle clean water upon you, and you shall be clean from all your uncleannesses, and from all your idols I will cleanse you. A new heart I will give you, and a new spirit I will put within you; and I will take out of your flesh the heart of stone and give you a heart of flesh. And I will put my spirit within you, and cause you to walk in my statutes and be careful to observe my ordinances. You shall dwell in the land which I gave to your fathers; and you shall be my people, and I will be your God." (Ezek. 36:25-28.)

The ultimate content, therefore, of the eschatological hope of the end of the age is found in the coming of God in power, to establish his sovereignty over Israel and the world. The Kingdom of God thus exceeds in scope its earlier identification with the Kingdom of Israel. The way is paved for the use made of this concept by Jesus and the church. The new age is pictured as a new creation. It is the old restored, yet it is new. It is more than a revival of that which has been; it is transformation and completion of the best in Israel's heritage. A great many of the details of this composite image of the future are ideal rather than realistic, they represent what *must* be rather than what shall be, they exhibit the prophetic hope and confidence in the ultimate triumph of the purpose and will of God for men. The question to be asked is, therefore, whether, and in what respect, such forecasts of the future may be expected to be realized in history, and in what ways the New Testament understanding of the church as the New Israel may be expected to pick up those elements appropriate to its work and mission, claiming fulfillment in a Christian context.

CHAPTER V

The Categories of Fulfillment

New Testament writers quote the Old Testament in two different ways. Sometimes references are by way of allusion, and sometimes citations are direct. Allusions are instances in which phrases are drawn from the Old Testament and used in such a way that New Testament teaching is framed in combinations of words known from other connections. This practice makes the reader feel that he is on familiar ground, and the thought is followed more readily. When complete citations are made, there is often the direct assertion that what was written in former times points the way to specific Christian doctrine and finds realization in the life and work of Christ and the church.

The letters of Paul make wide use of allusion. In speaking of God's blessing upon the righteous man, Paul quotes a psalm:

Blessed are those whose iniquities are forgiven, and whose sins
    are covered;
blessed is the man against whom the Lord will not reckon his sin.
                            (Rom. 4:7; cf. Ps. 32:1-2.)

Concerning the calling of the Gentiles to the faith, he paraphrases Hosea:

> Those who were not my people
> I will call "my people,"
> and her who was not beloved
> I will call "my beloved."
>   (Rom. 9:25.)

Of the man who is justified by faith, Paul selects appropriate phrases from Isa. 28:16, " No one who believes in him will be put to shame," and from Joel 2:32, " every one who calls upon the name of the Lord will be saved." (Rom. 10:11-13.) The wisdom of God is illustrated from Isa. 40:13-14:

> For who has known the mind of the Lord,
> or who has been his counselor?

and from Job 41:11:

> Or who has given a gift to him
> that he might be repaid?
> (Rom. 11:33-35.)

As to food offered to idols, Paul advises the Corinthians to respect the scruples of one's neighbor, but he also quotes Ps. 24:1: " The earth is the Lord's, and everything in it." (I Cor. 10:26.) Instances like this could be indefinitely multiplied. They illustrate the fact that Paul, as well as the author of The Letter to the Hebrews, and other New Testament writers, was steeped in the language of the Scriptures, and used familiar combinations of words to emphasize truths to which attention is directed. Allusions of this kind are found frequently in the New Testament books. Any idea that fulfillment is alleged would seem to be quite incidental.

The more significant type of quotation, so far as we are here concerned, is that in which a passage is recalled, and is now seen to have additional significance beyond its original content, or is observed to find realization along lines somewhat different from the original sense. In connecting Jesus with the Old Testament heritage, the New Testament writers contend that he is himself, in his person and by his work, bringing to fuller actuality many of the leading themes of the ancient faith of Israel. He is recognized as the fulfillment not only of one but of many Old Testament concepts. By claiming that Jesus is the realization of more than one Old Testament idea, a fusion takes place in the minds of many readers, resulting in a blurring of the distinctions origi-

nally existing among them. Thus, Christians hold that Jesus is the
expected Messiah, pictured by the prophets of old; that he is the
servant of the Lord, accomplishing what was ascribed to that figure in the latter part of The Book of Isaiah; that he is the ideal
prophet, " one from among you," as indicated in the Pentateuch;
that he is the great High Priest, fulfilling perfectly the office of
intercessor with the Father; that he is the sacrifice offered for the
sins of the world; that he is the Son of Man, coming on the
clouds in great glory.

The New Testament writers make each of these applications,
and because this is so, we are sometimes prone not to consider
the original aspects that distinguished these concepts each from
the other. We confuse the Old Testament idea of messiah with
that of suffering servant — did not Christ suffer? The well-
known hymn beginning " Crown him with many crowns " speaks
of " the Lamb upon his throne," though this is not an exact rem-
iniscence of the symbolism in Revelation. The ideas of God as
king and of the Lamb as sacrifice are fused because both of them
meet in the work of Christ. In order fully to appreciate the significance of these concepts claimed as fulfilled, let us consider
them separately, and attempt to discern exactly how each is seen
to find its culmination in the good news of Christ.

THE KINGLY MESSIAH

From the beginning of the preaching of the risen Lord, the
contention of the church was that " this Jesus, whom you have
crucified, is the Christ " (e.g., Acts 5:42: " Every day in the temple and at home they did not cease teaching and preaching Jesus
as the Christ ").

By so doing, Christians drew upon the whole range of Messianic
expectation that had developed through the years. The matured
theology of Israel understood that God should be considered as
the ruler of his people. His was the Kingdom, and Israel was his
people. Earthly kings that were anointed were subject to him, and
exercised authority on his behalf. Saul and David were called

"the Lord's anointed," for which the Hebrew word was "messiah." But the Kingdom was the Lord's.

One after another, David's successors fell short of accomplishing what was implied by this conception. They showed themselves inadequate to the tasks that confronted them. Israel and Judah began to feel the pressure exerted by threat of foreign invaders. A succession of crises disturbed the peace and well-being of the people. A longing arose, quite understandably, that somehow these perils would cease and stability would ensue. A hope was entertained among the people that the day was speedily approaching when the Lord would intervene decisively in the course of human history, would triumph over the heathen, exalt his own people, and inaugurate a new era of prosperity, righteousness, and peace. In so doing, he would truly be King over all the earth. Thus there grew the concept of a kingdom of God, though this combination of words does not actually occur in the Old Testament in this form.

Hope for the future originated, naturally, in human desire for a full life, but more especially it was fostered by the understanding that there was a covenant relation between God and his people. It was popularly assumed that because of this relationship, men could confidently look for the realization of the Kingdom of God in joyful anticipation. It remained for the prophets rudely to disturb this complacency with their messages of judgment. They boldly announced that men must meet the demands of righteousness, justice, and repentance before any such expectation could become an actuality.

Connected with the rule of God over his people, there was sometimes associated the hope that an ideal ruler would exercise authority on behalf of the Lord, in accordance with the principle under which the kingdom had come into being under Saul and David. For this reason, after the close of the Old Testament the term "messianic" came to be used to designate the rule of God in the coming age, though this usage does not appear in the Old Testament itself. Nowhere in its pages is the ideal earthly

king called "messiah." Some other term is always used. It occurs for the first time in the noncanonical literature of later
Judaism.

The prophets do not always include a messianic earthly ruler
in their forecasts of the golden age. There is no mention of a
messiah in the second and third chapters of Zephaniah, where
the coming of the sovereignty of God is described at length, or
in Isa., chs. 24 to 27, a succession of oracles revolving around this
theme. Rather, the Lord is King, exercising direct authority,
judging, redeeming, and teaching his people. The same is true of
the description of the new age in the poem in Isa. 54:11-17, and
in chs. 55 and 56. The idea of a messiah is therefore subordi-
nate to the wider conception of the Kingdom of God. In the
absence of such a representative, authority is exercised by God
himself.

On other occasions, the prophets included in their forecasts delineations of the kind of earthly king who, in their formulations,
would participate in the coming age. Observing the shortcomings
of the reign of Zedekiah, Jeremiah gave the following description: "Behold, the days are coming, says the Lord, when I will
raise up for David a righteous Branch, and he shall reign as king
and deal wisely, and shall execute justice and righteousness in the
land. In his days Judah will be saved, and Israel will dwell se-
curely. And this is the name by which he will be called: 'The
Lord is our righteousness.'" (Jer. 23:5-6.) This appears to be a
play upon the name of Zedekiah, which means "righteousness of
the Lord." The ideal king truly will be what was suggested by
the name, but what was not true of the reigning monarch.

With the fall of Judah and the end of the Davidic dynasty, the
expectation of a restoration of the house of David assumed more
significance. Ezekiel pictures God as the shepherd of his people:
"I myself will be the shepherd of my sheep, and I will make them
lie down, says the Lord God. I will seek the lost, and I will bring
back the strayed, and I will bind up the crippled, and I will
strengthen the weak, and the fat and the strong I will watch

over; I will feed them in justice. . . . I, the Lord, will be their God, and my servant David shall be prince among them." (Ezek. 34:15-16, 24.) A later addition to The Book of Amos looks for the revival of the house of David: "In that day I will raise up the booth of David that is fallen and repair its breaches, and raise up its ruins, and rebuild it as in the days of old; that they may possess the remnant of Edom and all the nations who are called by my name." (Amos 9:11-12.)

Passages in the preexilic prophets that imply a restoration of the dynasty of David are considered by many scholars to have been modified after the exile to adapt them to this idea, which of course later would be necessary. While Judah was still independent, there would be no need for a restoration. Rather, the preexilic prophecies point to a day when the existing dynasty would eventuate in a king who would exemplify the ideal. Thus we have the classic pictures in Isaiah in which the king is described in these terms:

> . . . his name will be called
> "Wonderful Counselor, Mighty God,
>   Everlasting Father, Prince of Peace."
> Of the increase of his government and of peace
>   there will be no end,
> upon the throne of David, and over his kingdom,
>   to establish it, and to uphold it
> with justice and with righteousness
>   from this time forth and for evermore.
>
> (Isa. 9:6-7.)

Again,

> . . . the Spirit of the Lord shall rest upon him,
>   the spirit of wisdom and understanding,
>   the spirit of counsel and might,
>   the spirit of knowledge and the fear of the Lord.
>
> (Isa. 11:2.)

He is further represented as having others associated with him in his government:

> Behold, a king will reign in righteousness,
>   and princes will rule in justice.
> Each will be like a hiding place from the wind,
>   a covert from the tempest,
> like streams of water in a dry place,
>   like the shade of a great rock in a weary land.
>
> (Isa. 32:1-2.)

Thus righteousness and faithfulness are characteristics of the era of the ideal king, and protection extends to all who need it. Security and peace prevail, whose blessing extends figuratively even to the animal world, so that

> The wolf shall dwell with the lamb,
>   and the leopard shall lie down with the kid,
> and the calf and the lion and the fatling together,
> . . . .
> They shall not hurt or destroy
>   in all my holy mountain;
> for the earth shall be full of the knowledge of the Lord
>   as the waters cover the sea.
>
> (Isa. 11:6, 9.)

From these and similar passages, it will be seen that a characteristic circle of ideas came to be associated with the reign of the anticipated Messiah. It was thought of as connected with the "Day of the Lord," the end of the age, either as heralding that day or as being established by the arrival of the day. It was pictured in terms of political rule — the kingly office would thus come into its own, and authority would be exercised not alone over God's kingdom in Israel but over the foreign nations as well. Those who had long oppressed Israel would now become subject to the rule of Israel and her Messiah. Justice, righteousness, victory, peace, and prosperity would be characteristics of the age, thus fulfilling the ancient hopes of the nation. After the canon of the prophets was closed, about 200 B.C., the Messianic expectation continued to be emphasized in the noncanonical literature, with the same recurrent themes, so that when Jesus preached the Kingdom of God as at hand, it was natural that many of his hearers would associate with the phrase the circle of ideas which had so long clustered about it.

But Jesus did not consider his mission to be political. The disciples of John came to him asking, " Are you he who is to come, or shall we look for another? " The reply of Jesus was significant: " Go and tell John what you hear and see: the blind receive their sight and the lame walk, lepers are cleansed and the deaf hear, and the dead are raised up, and the poor have good news preached to them." (Matt. 11:3-5.) Yet he constantly proclaimed that the Kingdom of God was being realized. He never claimed for himself the title of messiah, and when Peter applied it to him at Caesarea Philippi, " he strictly charged the disciples to tell no one that he was the Christ " (Matt. 16:20).

Nevertheless, after the resurrection, the proclamation of Jesus as the Messiah became the central and characteristic assertion of the gospel. That in him there had come to pass the essential elements of the Messianic expectation was the essence of the apostolic preaching. The presence of God in power, the redemption of the people, the proclamation of righteousness and justice, the emphasis on humility and character rather than on political or military supremacy, was set forth as evidence of the Lordship of Jesus. The term " Christ " (i.e., " Messiah "), which was properly a title, then came to be used as the name of the risen Lord. All this stressed the belief that fulfillment had come about, but it was in terms other than those originally set forth in the Prophets and the Psalms. This reinterpretation is of the essence of Christian understanding of the work of Jesus. He is seen as the King, not of a reconstituted nation of Israel, but of the so-called Israel of God, a kingdom that knows no boundaries and is not limited to those who traced descent through the twelve tribes. The kingdom thus comes to be universal rather than national, and the kingship no longer partakes of those military and administrative elements that comprise the terminology in which the Old Testament pictures it. The throne is not one located in Jerusalem, as had been anticipated, but a spiritual throne over the lives of those who understand, who become the new Zion. The contention of the New Testament is that Jesus *fulfills* the expectation of the kingly Messiah.

THE SON OF MAN

If Jesus never is recorded as having called himself " Messiah," quite the opposite is the case with the title " the Son of Man." He is reported to have used the phrase repeatedly of himself. It is found in all the Gospels, practically from beginning to end, and characteristically is used in sayings of Jesus about himself or by the Gospel writers who attribute its use to him. Such wide use indicates that it conveyed a meaning that he considered appropriate and that was considered significant by the evangelists.

As an Old Testament phrase, it is characteristic of Ezekiel, who calls himself " son of man " no fewer than ninety times. By it the prophet meant to contrast his own frail humanity with the might and eternity of God. As a son of man, he identified himself with his fellow exiles and shared their weaknesses. He was a mere human being. A similar meaning is called up by the use of the phrase in two of the psalms, in which the identical questions are asked,

> What is man that thou art mindful of him,
>   and the son of man that thou dost care for him?
> (Ps. 8:4; 144:3.)

In the parallelism, " son of man " is equivalent to " mortal man." The double answer of the psalms is that man is feeble and transitory, here today and gone tomorrow, yet made in the likeness of God and partaking of nobility for this reason. Frailty is similarly indicated when the words are used in Num. 23:19; Job 35:8;

Ps. 80:17; 146:3; and Isa. 51:12; 56:2.

A different meaning is found in the seventh chapter of Daniel. This chapter contains a vision of four beasts that come up out of the sea. They represent four kingdoms which successively have dominion over the earth. In all probability they are the Babylonian, Persian, Greek, and Syrian kingdoms, which in turn ruled that part of the world which included the scattered people of Israel. Then the vision continues,

As for the rest of the beasts, their dominion was taken away, but their lives were prolonged for a season and a time. I saw in the night visions,

> and behold, with the clouds of heaven
> there came one like a son of man,
> and he came to the Ancient of Days
> and was presented before him.
> And to him was given dominion
> and glory and kingdom,
> that all peoples, nations, and languages
> should serve him;
> his dominion is an everlasting dominion,
> which shall not pass away,
> and his kingdom one
> that shall not be destroyed.

(Dan. 7:12-14.)

Later in the chapter an interpretation is given, in which it is indicated that

> . . . the greatness of the kingdoms under the whole heaven
> shall be given to the people of the saints of the Most High;
> their kingdom shall be an everlasting kingdom,
> and all dominions shall serve and obey them.

(Dan. 7:27.)

It would appear, then, that in The Book of Daniel the " son of man " is " the saints of the Most High," that is, those who have acknowledged God as the only ruler, and who have acted in accordance with that acknowledgment.

The instances given are the only examples of the appearance of these words in the Old Testament. But the New Testament usage certainly does not rest upon these alone. In the nearly two centuries that elapsed between the composition of The Book of Daniel and the reported sayings of Jesus, the idea of the Son of Man developed in a remarkable way which alone can explain the use made of the phrase by the writers of the Gospels. A new content came into the words that is not reflected in the Old Testament, but that is necessary to explain what the words meant to people in New Testament times.

The Book of Enoch, which survives in an Ethiopic translation of a Hebrew and Aramaic work of the first two pre-Christian centuries, describes an Elect One, or Chosen One, in whose days righteousness shall prevail, and in whose presence the elect or chosen people will remain forever. This is perhaps a further personification of the figure in Daniel, and it is said that he will sit on the throne of glory, and " try the works " of the righteous. He is characterized by the spirit of wisdom, understanding, and might, the same qualities which we noted as ascribed to the Messiah by the prophet. Yet this figure is seemingly not identified with the Messiah in The Book of Enoch, but rather equated with the Son of Man, who is described later. The Son of Man is said to remove from their thrones the kings and the mighty ones who have persecuted the saints. All judgment is committed to him. He was hidden from the beginning, but is revealed by God to his elect ones. It appears to many scholars that this symbolic figure stands behind the phraseology of the Gospels, and recognition of this fact is essential to any understanding of the meaning that the words conveyed when used by the New Testament writers.

Jesus seems to have had at least two kinds of meaning in mind in his reported use of the phrase. Some of his sayings equate the meaning with the Old Testament sense of " mere human," as in Luke 6:5, " The Son of man is lord of the sabbath," and Mark

2:10-11, "But that you may know that the Son of man has authority on earth to forgive sins . . . I say to you, rise, take up your pallet and go home." These examples speak of unexpected authority on the part of mere man. But there are other sayings in which is clearly reflected the kind of background that we have noted in The Book of Enoch: The Son of Man comes in clouds with great power and glory, to gather his elect from the ends of heaven (Mark 13:26-27; Matt. 24:30; Luke 21:27). He came not to be served but to serve, and to give his life as a ransom for many (Mark 10:45; Matt. 20:28; Luke 22:27). It is recorded that Jesus "began to teach them that the Son of man must suffer many things, and be rejected by the elders and the chief priests and the scribes, and be killed, and after three days rise again" (Mark 8:31; see also Mark 9:31 and ch. 10:33-34).

In the Gospel of John, both the human and the otherworldly aspects are again apparent. John 1:51 speaks of angels ascending and descending upon the Son of Man — perhaps an allusion to the baptism. Other passages seem to imply preexistence of the Son of Man in heaven, his coming into the world as the bread of life (John 6:27, 32, 53), and his return to heaven (John 3:13).

Outside the Gospels, the phrase occurs only as spoken by Stephen at his martyrdom (Acts 7:56) and in symbolic passages in Revelation, where there seems to be an allusion to its usage in Daniel (Rev. 1:13; 14:14). Paul never uses the words "Son of Man," but he may have it in mind in his contrast of the first Adam with the Second Adam (Rom. 5:14-19; I Cor. 15:21-23, 45-50), since the name "Adam" means "man."

The New Testament application to Jesus of the title "Son of Man" clearly means to indicate that Jesus is the fulfillment of the different concepts that this phrase connoted. On the one hand he was a frail human, like all the rest of mankind. He was subject to hunger, thirst, fatigue, suffering, and death, as are all men. He is one with humanity in his incarnation. On the other hand the title carries the triumphant note of eternal exaltation; the Son of Man who is betrayed into the hands of sinners comes again in triumph in the clouds of heaven, to sit at the right hand of Power. This is not a picture of the Messianic King, but is a separate and distinct figure, which had acquired a prominence after the close of the Old Testament, and which Jesus adopted with reference to himself, in preference to the term " Messiah." The New Testament contention is that in Jesus of Nazareth there is fulfillment of the concept of the Son of Man.

THE IDEAL PROPHET

The Old Testament prophet was essentially an interpreter of life in terms of the understanding of the ways of God with men. He looked to the past, examining critically the significance of what had occurred. He looked to the present, judging contemporary situations, attitudes, purposes, and motives, and bringing to bear upon them the moral requirements of the divine demand concerning human activities. He looked to the future, to portray what must be the goals of life, and the ends toward which men must strive. The prophets did not so much predict what was going to happen as portray the kind of future that must come about if God is truly supreme over his world. The basic task of the prophet was to set forth for his hearers the character of God and the response that men must make to him, in the light of their understanding of him and his ways.

It is in this way that we discern the role of Jesus as the ideal prophet. He came that men might have life, and have it abundantly (John 10:10). He came to make known what God is truly like: " If you had known me, you would have known my Father also; henceforth you know him and have seen him." (John 14:7.) In his concern for others, in his discernment of true values, in his submission to his Father's purposes (" Not my will, but thine, be done " [Luke 22:42]) he set forth the true nature of God and exhibited the perfect following of God's will. Just as Isaiah, Jeremiah, and the other prophets of old had striven to express the divine requirements to men, so Jesus set forth anew the will of God for his people. The prophet was a spokesman for God. So also was our Lord, in a very real way.

It is perhaps remarkable that the New Testament writers and the preachers of the early church did not really apply the term "prophet" to Jesus. This is the more surprising, inasmuch as they recognized him as in line with the great teachers of Israel. The references to him as prophet were almost always recorded as the judgment of some person or group of people who had heard him speak or seen him do some mighty work. Thus the Samaritan woman at the well said, "Sir, I perceive that you are a prophet" (John 4:19). The blind man whose sight was restored said to the Pharisees, "He is a prophet" (John 9:17). On other occasions it appears to have been a designation by a larger group. Matthew noted that the chief priests and the Pharisees heard his parables and perceived that he was speaking about them, "but when they tried to arrest him, they feared the multitudes, because they held him to be a prophet" (Matt. 21:46). At Nain the people, seeing his mighty work among them, exclaimed, "A great prophet has arisen among us!" and, "God has visited his people!" (Luke 7:16.) Of the reactions of those who heard him preach, John records that "some of the people said, 'This is really the prophet.' Others said, 'This is the Christ.' But some said, 'Is the Christ to come from Galilee?'" (John 7:40-41.)

Jesus was called a prophet by those who saw him feed the five thousand (John 6:14), and by the crowds on the occasion of his entry into Jerusalem on Palm Sunday when they said, "This is the prophet Jesus from Nazareth of Galilee" (Matt. 21:11). When Jesus asked his disciples at Caesarea Philippi, "Who do men say that I am?" they answered, "John the Baptist; and others say, Elijah; and others one of the prophets." (Mark 8:27-28; cf. Matt. 16:13-14; Luke 9:18-19.) We further note that the two disciples on the road to Emmaus, when asked about recent events by the as yet unknown traveler who had joined them, replied that they spoke "concerning Jesus of Nazareth, who was a prophet mighty in deed and word before God and all the people," but who had been condemned to death and crucified (Luke 24:19).

There is no record that Jesus ever used the word "prophet" of himself, unless we find it in his proverbial remark, recorded in all four Gospels: " A prophet is not without honor, except in his own country, and among his own kin, and in his own house " (Mark 6:4 and parallels); or in his statement in sending forth the twelve disciples: " He who receives you receives me, and he who receives me receives him who sent me. He who receives a prophet because he is a prophet shall receive a prophet's reward, and he who receives a righteous man because he is a righteous man shall receive a righteous man's reward " (Matt. 10:40-41). Furthermore, whereas Paul has much to say in his epistles about prophecy in the church and the true spirit of prophecy, he never applied the word to Christ, but preferred other designations.

In connection with the early witness of Peter and Stephen (Acts 3:22-23; 7:37), the words of Deuteronomy are quoted: " The Lord your God will raise up for you a prophet like me from among you, from your brethren — him you shall heed." (Deut. 18:15.) They imply that at long last Jesus has become this prophet, anticipated since the very beginning. However, the original passage in Deuteronomy does not really refer to a particular person, but to a long succession of prophets who were destined to be the teachers of Israel. The chapter discusses true and false prophets, and sets forth that when Moses is no longer the living teacher of his people, to guide them in the observance of the covenant relationship with God, they are not to be left leaderless, but from time to time " a prophet " will arise among them who will perform the function assumed by Moses. The use of the word " prophet " in the singular, to designate an indefinite number of individuals in succession, is exactly parallel to the phrase in the preceding chapter (Deut. 17:14-15): " When you come to the land . . . and dwell in it, and then say, ' I will set a king over me, like all the nations that are round about me '; you may indeed set as king over you him whom the Lord your God will choose." The reference here is not to a particular king, a Saul or a David or a Solomon, but to the office of kingship; similarly the reference in the following chapter is to the prophetic office rather than to a particular person. There appears to have been no precedent in previous Jewish usage for the kind of application implied by Peter and Stephen in their quotation of this ancient pronouncement, or in their application of it to the risen Lord.

The Letter to the Hebrews begins by contrasting God's word through the prophets with his revelation in Christ: " In many and various ways God spoke of old to our fathers by the prophets; but in these last days he has spoken to us by a Son." (Heb. 1:1-2.) In The Revelation to John the message of Jesus and the phenomenon of prophecy are brought together: " For the testimony of Jesus is the spirit of prophecy." (Rev. 19:10.)

The real claim of the church is not that men called Jesus a prophet, still less that he was given to making predictions, but rather that by his life and work he made known the character and ways of God. As the seers and spokesmen of old had set forth the many facets of God's dealings with his people, so Jesus made clearer than ever before the truth concerning the Father and the meaning of true obedience on the part of his children. In this sense he properly may be spoken of as the true prophet, and the creeds of the church properly have held that Jesus is Prophet, Priest, and King.

PERFECT PRIEST AND PERFECT SACRIFICE

The New Testament further identifies Jesus as the consummation of the idea of priesthood. In Old Testament times, the function of the priest was in vivid contrast to that of the prophet. The role of the prophet was to stand before God and plead God's case with men. The role of the priest was to stand before men and plead their case with God. The prophet took his position on the side of God with reference to his people. The priest took his position on the side of the people in relation to their God.

The idea of priesthood is very ancient, but its development throughout the course of the Old Testament is somewhat obscure. The conventional view, as set forth in the tradition of the Pentateuch, is that Moses originated the institution, assigning priestly duties to the tribe of Levi. Aaron the Levite is represented as the typical priest, and elaborate rituals are set forth for the performance of his duties. The office of priest was hereditary, but the descendants of Aaron himself were considered as the priests par excellence, and others of the tribe were assigned subsidiary duties. The distinction among the three orders — high priest, priest, and Levite — is thus carried back to the wilderness.

Modern scholarship is of the opinion that this is an oversimplification of the situation. What is represented here is a later development of the worship of Israel, reflected back by tradition to the beginnings. In the early period the priest was not concerned merely with sacrifice. He was considered to be an instrument of the revelation of God, and in this capacity gave instruction and guidance in the ordinary affairs of life. It would seem that the teaching function of the priest actually took precedence over the sacrificial. According to the traditional Blessing of Moses, the destiny of Levi puts teaching first:

> They shall teach Jacob thy ordinances,
>   and Israel thy law;
> they shall put incense before thee,
>   and whole burnt offering upon thy altar.
>   (Deut. 33:10.)

As a successor to Moses, the priest gave oracular direction. He was entrusted with responsibilty for legal decision on the basis of precedent, and even in the case of some conditions of illness, he had authority to declare a person clean or unclean. No doubt the worship at the Tabernacle in the wilderness was relatively simple; certainly at a later date, when Eli and his sons were the custodians of the Ark of the Covenant at Shiloh, no elaborate hierarchy or ritual prevailed. It was with the development of the Temple in Jerusalem, built as a royal shrine in the time of Solomon, that ceremonies and more highly developed cultic activities came into their own.

In early times, sacrifice was not limited to performance by

priests. The patriarchs, Abraham, Isaac, and Jacob, performed this rite in their capacity as heads of the household. Numerous instances in the books of Judges, Samuel, and Kings record occasions when sacrifice was offered by the father of a house, a judge, a king, a prophet, or others. Samuel himself, not a Levite but an Ephraimite, officiated at the altar on occasion. Evidently the elaborate ritual described in the so-called books of Moses is a description of forms that developed over the years, later set down as standard, and ascribed to Moses himself.

Israel is represented as chosen by God and therefore under an obligation to holiness. The original meaning of " holy " is " set apart," " separated," and was applied to places, to objects, to ordinances, and to persons. " For you are a people holy to the Lord your God; the Lord your God has chosen you to be a people for his own possession, out of all the peoples that are on the face of the earth." (Deut. 7:6.) " You shall be holy; for I the Lord your God am holy." (Lev. 19:2.) The law lays upon the Levitical priesthood the responsibility for custodianship of this tradition.

The function of the priesthood was therefore to assure, maintain, and constantly reestablish the holiness of the chosen people. Through the priesthood, Israel was thought to be purified and sanctified, prepared to serve God and receive his blessing. The priest became the mediator of the covenant with God.

This is the basic principle that in the New Testament is claimed to reach its culmination and fulfillment in Christ. He is called the great High Priest, one with the Father through his eternal Sonship, yet by his incarnation identified with men. Hence he is the perfect Mediator of the New Covenant, who has once for all made atonement for sin and opened for men a new and living way into the presence of God. This concept is set forth uniquely in The Letter to the Hebrews.

It seems quite probable that this letter was written as an extended discussion, or theological treatise, on the subject of man's approach to God through Christ. It was probably not a letter in the sense in which Paul's letters were addressed to particular recipients. It presupposes a situation in which the Hebrew Christians were in danger of spiritual immaturity: "You need milk, not solid food; for every one who lives on milk is unskilled in the word of righteousness, for he is a child. But solid food is for the mature, for those who have their faculties trained by practice to distinguish good from evil." (Heb. 5:12-14.)

This maturity of experience is said to be brought about by full understanding and acceptance of the priesthood of Christ, which is thus associated with spiritual steadfastness, progress, and assurance. It is evident that the readers had a knowledge of Jesus as Savior, and had an elementary understanding of the truths of redemption, but they did not know what it meant to have him as priest. Priesthood provides the means of access to God and does away with fear in approaching him. It is based on an already existing redemption.

This is the distinction between the teaching of Paul in his letter to the Romans and the teaching of the author of Hebrews. Paul is concerned with redemption which makes access possible (Rom. 5:2). Hebrews is concerned with access which is made possible by redemption. Jesus is called "the apostle and high priest of our confession" (Heb. 3:1). In this one phrase, the author speaks of him in his office as prophet ("apostle" means "one sent") and as priest, linking together these two ideas. But the priesthood spoken of is identified, not with the Levitical priesthood of the Pentateuch but with the symbolic priesthood of Melchizedek, the half-legendary king of Salem to whom Abraham gave gifts. Melchizedek, whose name means "king of righteousness," is seen to typify Christ in three ways: first, in his royalty, as king; second, in the righteousness suggested by his name; and third, in peace, because "Salem," of which he was said to be king, has this meaning. Whereas the Levitical priesthood was hereditary, Melchizedek appears on the scene in the Abraham story, then disappears, so that Hebrews describes him as "without father or mother or genealogy," and having "neither beginning of days nor end of life, but resembling the Son of God he continues a priest for ever" (Heb. 7:1-3).

In this letter, therefore, the person of Christ is presented as the consummation of the priestly office of the Old Testament. He is at once the sinless High Priest and also the unblemished sacrifice, making forever unnecessary the sacrifice of bulls or rams or goats. He supplants the ancient ritual with that for which it stood: the provision of means of access to the grace of God through faith in Christ.

Priesthood is not ascribed to our Lord in other parts of the New Testament, but there are echoes of the sacrificial character of his death and resurrection in many places. In Mark 10:45 he himself said he had come "to give his life as a ransom for many." At the Last Supper he spoke of his "blood of the covenant, which is poured out for many" (Mark 14:24). Paul speaks of Christ as the Paschal lamb which has been sacrificed (I Cor. 5:7) and as an offering for sin (Rom. 8:3). Paul regards him as one "whom God put forward as an expiation by his blood, to be received by faith" (Rom. 3:25). He is called "The Lamb of God, who takes away the sin of the world" (John 1:29); and, in the book of Revelation, myriads of thousands cry out, "Worthy is the Lamb who was slain, to receive power and wealth and wisdom and might and honor and glory and blessing!" (Rev. 5:12.) Thus Jesus is set forth by the New Testament as the fulfillment of two complementary Old Testament figures: he is said to be the perfect priest, and at the same time the unblemished sacrifice. The fulfillment claimed, however, is not because of priestly activities during his earthly life, nor because of the manner of his death, but by reason of who he is, and what his incarnation, death, and resurrection mean to men. The priesthood of Aaron passed away once and for all, and with it the animal sacrifices so closely associated as part of it, for Christ is understood to have become the mediator between man and God, thus fulfilling two roles, that of priest and that of completed sacrifice.

The Servant of the Lord

Perhaps the most significant of Old Testament figures claimed to be fulfilled by Jesus is that of the Servant of the Lord. This

magnificent conception is found chiefly in chs. 41 to 53 of The
Book of Isaiah. It is associated with two other themes: God's man-
ifestation in power of himself, beside whom there is no other, and
the impending deliverance of the exiles by the raising up of Cy-
rus the Persian. God has chosen Israel, calling the people from
the ends of the earth, and saying,

> . . . You are my servant,
> I have chosen you and not cast you off.
> (Isa. 41:9.)

The exiles are therefore to take heart and try to understand the
meaning of the divine redemption that is at hand.

The word " servant " basically means " slave," but it has also a
wider meaning; when used in connection with the name of a
deity, it is really equivalent to "worshiper." " His servants the
prophets " is a phrase used more than once (II Kings 9:7; Ezra
9:11; Amos 3:7), the patriarchs are similarly designated, and
Moses is called God's servant no fewer than thirty-six times (e.g.,
Ex. 14:31). To serve the Lord is to honor him and to act in accordance with his will. But the phrase comes uniquely into its
own in the use made of it in The Book of Isaiah.

Beginning with the designation of Israel as the servant of the
Lord, a series of poems delineates the character of this personification, describes the mission assigned to him, and indicates the
manner of his carrying out that mission. In speaking of the national group as a personification, the poet uses personal terms
with respect to it.

> " You are my witnesses," says the Lord,
> " and my servant whom I have chosen,
> that you may know and believe me
> and understand that I am He.
> Before me no god was formed,
> nor shall there be any after me."
> (Isa. 43:10.)

Yet the description is given in increasingly personal terms as the chapters proceed, so that many have seen a transfer from the idea of the nation to an ideal Israel, whose mission is to gather the whole people to the Lord, and the prophetic voice further in some passages identifies the servant with himself.

Whether in the sequence the prophet moves in his representation from the whole people through the ideal kernel within the nation and on to an individual, or whether the concept of corporate personality accounts for the apparent progression, the fact remains that the redemption of the people is somehow brought about through the career of the servant, including the fact that he suffers ill treatment and sickness on their behalf. A wide variety of suggestions has been made through the years in attempts to identify exactly who it was that the prophet had in mind, ranging all the way from the prophet himself through specific persons in Israel's history to the representation of a future personage who might be expected to come.

Although repeatedly it has been so stated, it seems that the servant can hardly be the kingly Messiah. A king is not a slave, and a servant does not exercise regal authority. This is a separate concept, independent of the Messianic idea in its strict definition. The fact that the New Testament sees our Lord as the fulfillment of the servant idea, and also sees him as Messiah, has resulted in confusing two concepts that properly ought to be distinguished.

The servant is represented as God's chosen one, on whom he has put his spirit. In humility and faithfulness he is obedient to the task set before him. Although he is portrayed as blind and deaf, not understanding fully his mission, yet he is the witness to the uniqueness of God the Creator, the Holy One of Israel; he is also to be a light to the nations, that God's salvation may reach to the ends of the earth. So his character and career are further described, and though despised and forsaken by men, stricken for the transgression of his people, he is brought by the Lord to final victory and exaltation.

> . . . he poured out his soul to death,
>   and was numbered with the transgressors;
> yet he bore the sin of many,
>   and made intercession for the transgressors.
>   (Isa. 53:12.)

Small wonder it is that the New Testament writers find in Jesus the fulfillment of the idea of the servant of the Lord. He too came to bear witness to the one true God. He too performed with quiet dedication the tasks set before him, opening the way for God's redemptive purpose, not only toward his chosen people but toward all the nations of the world. His was the chastisement that makes us whole, and with his stripes we are healed. So it is that one after another of the Gospels, as well as the letters, make wide use of this comparison, and see in our Lord the realization in fact of the work ascribed by the prophet to the servant. Phrases from the servant songs are echoed in almost every part of the New Testament.

A typical use is suggested by the incident recorded of the conversation of Philip with the Ethiopian traveler on the road to Gaza (Acts 8:26-40). Being invited to come and sit in the chariot, Philip found the traveler reading the passage:

> As a sheep led to the slaughter
> or a lamb before its shearer is dumb,
> so he opens not his mouth.
> In his humiliation justice was denied him.
> Who can describe his generation?
> For his life is taken up from the earth.

The question was asked of Philip, "About whom, pray, does the prophet say this, about himself or about some one else?" This, of course, is the age-old question. We are not told the particular answer that Philip gave, but "beginning with this scripture he told him the good news of Jesus."

Philip's use of the passage is correct. Whoever may have been intended in the original passage, the idea that redemption comes through the uncomplaining suffering of one on behalf of others is the very heart of the Christian message. This is the principle that Jesus made incarnate. The poetic representation of the prophet finds actuality and realization in the work of Christ. In him is seen true fulfillment.

THE NEW COVENANT

The most comprehensive instance of fulfillment claimed for an Old Testament figure is found in the message of the Christian gospel itself. It is termed the New Covenant between God and man. Based on the passage in Jer. 31:31-34, it is set forth as marking the distinction between the old era and the new, between the pre-Christian understanding of God's dealings with his people and the new relationship made possible and explicit in Christ.

Jeremiah had called attention to the old covenant, made with the fathers when they were brought out of Egypt and emphasized in the experience at Sinai. It was that the Lord would be their God, and they would be his people. Experience showed that the covenant had been broken by the willful disobedience of human nature, but that God wished it to prevail. So the prophet gave assurance that a new covenant would be made with the house of Israel and the house of Judah. Unlike the old, its law would be written not on tables of stone but on the human heart, not as an external requirement but as an inner compulsion. It would be universal: there would be no need for one to exhort another to know the Lord, for all should know him, from the least to the greatest. Furthermore, it would be made possible through the forgiveness of sin: "I will remember their sin no more." (Jer. 31:34.)

It is the contention of the New Testament that in Christ this new condition, pictured by the prophet, has come to reality. The author of The Letter to the Hebrews compares and contrasts the mediation that has come about through Christ with that which formerly prevailed. He quotes the entire section from Jeremiah

(Heb. 8:8-12), indicating that "what is becoming obsolete and growing old is ready to vanish away" (v. 13). He then describes the regulations that characterized Old Testament worship and the sacrifices that took place on the altar, but makes the point that now Christ has offered himself as a sacrifice, to enable men to serve the living God, and that thus he mediates a new covenant. "For by a single offering he has perfected for all time those who are sanctified." (Heb. 10:14.) Thus it is possible for us to approach God in full assurance of faith. This is the essence of the Christian gospel.

In telling of the way in which Jesus partook of the Last Supper with his disciples, Paul records that the Lord broke the bread, and said, "This is my body which is for you" (I Cor. 11:24). In the same way he also took the cup, saying: "This cup is the new covenant in my blood. Do this, as often as you drink it, in remembrance of me." (V. 25.) The repeated observance of the Lord's Supper is thus a repeated reminder of the fulfillment of Jeremiah's words in the work of Christ.

How appropriate it is, therefore, that the title page of the New Testament, in the Revised Standard Version, gives the following comprehensive designation to the books that tell the Christian message: "The New Covenant, commonly called the New Testament, of our Lord and Savior Jesus Christ." The words of Jeremiah have become for us the most all-inclusive name for the gospel.

Summary

The Christian message is summed up in the person of the risen Lord. His continuing presence with those who have eyes of faith to recognize him is the power that motivates his church. He is himself the good news of God's mercy and forgiveness. A new life is possible through him. The Bible is an interpretation of man's life under divine sovereignty: the essential error of ways that are exclusively human, resulting in a need for divine correction, and the ends that come to pass when men respond to the means of redemption provided. The great voices of Old Testament times expressed through the Law, the Prophets, and the Psalms the principles discernible in God's relationship with men. The New Testament shows how these have reached fuller vindication and application in Christ. No wonder the key word is "fulfillment." The goal of what went before is made objective in Christian experience. The hopes of earlier generations have reached a point of realization. What is accomplished corresponds with what had been anticipated, though in terms somewhat different from what had been expected.

The essential Christian position is one of fulfillment rather than of prediction. The New Testament makes citations from all parts of the Old. Jesus is recognized as kingly Messiah, as Son of Man, as ideal prophet, as perfect priest, as effective sacrifice, as servant of the Lord. In him the new covenant has come to actuality. The representations of former years have received corroboration and verification.

But this is not quite the same as asserting that the career of Jesus was described in advance, in ways that embody miraculous foresight. Fulfillment is claimed for much that was never prediction in the first place. The gospel is far more significant than any foretelling of it possibly could be. *The marvel is not that any prophet foretold. The marvel is that Jesus fulfills.* The wonder is not in any forecast of the future. The wonder is in the consummation that has come about because of Christ. To glorify prediction rather than fulfillment is to misunderstand the nature of the forecast, and to miss the significance of the Christian gospel.

Matthew, Mark, and Luke all record how Jesus, accompanied by Peter, James, and John, went to a high mountain and was there transfigured before them. This remarkable incident is significant for the insight it affords into our problem. Painters have tried to portray it, sermons have been preached about it, yet it has been so misrepresented and misunderstood that it has become unreal and unbelievable for many. The simplest account is in Mark. With his companions, Jesus led the way upward. We may be confident that as they climbed Jesus was in conversation with the others. What would have been the subject of their discussion? As was certainly true on other comparable occasions, they must have talked over the things that were uppermost in their minds. No doubt these had to do with his mission and their responsibility regarding it. If so, it involved the meaning of his life and teaching as part of the age-old revelation of God to men. Presently " he was transfigured before them," his garments appearing glistening white. " And there appeared to them Elijah with Moses; and they were talking to Jesus." Peter suggested that they make three booths, one for Jesus, one for Moses, and one for Elijah. Then a voice was heard, saying: " ' This is my beloved Son; listen to him.' And suddenly looking around they no longer saw any one with them but Jesus only." (Mark 9:2-8.)

The disciples suddenly perceived their Lord in a new light. It dawned upon them that he was indeed the fulfillment of the great tradition of the past. Moses and Elijah were the two figures that stood for that tradition. Moses had always been connected with the law; Elijah had for generations been the one who typified the prophets. They saw Jesus as standing with the law and the prophets, and the illumination resulting from this realization made him radiant in their eyes. They saw him as they had never seen him before. The mission of which he had been talking to them during their climb was now seen as rooted in what had been their heritage and that of their fathers before them. In him it was brought to accomplishment. Until now they had been instructed through the law and the prophets; now the realization came: " This is my beloved Son; listen to him." Moses and Elijah disappeared from the scene. They saw Jesus only. He had become their authority.

This representation of the scene on the mountain is the way the church understands the place of Christ in the course of God's revelation of himself to men. Through lawgivers and prophets and psalmists, insights and understandings have been expressed, all part of the truth made known to humankind. Among these insights are supreme teachings, forever valid, even if there had been no New Testament to reinforce them, verify them, and extend upon them. But with the coming of a superior teacher in the person of Jesus, through whom we perceive the world's clearest revelation of the Father, we recognize the former teachers as having prepared the way for him. Or, to change the figure of speech, they have been the guides who have led men to the feet of Christ to be taught by him.

This is precisely the contention of Paul in his letter to the Galatians. He shows how, under former conditions, the law provided a means by which to live; but now that Christ has come, the life of faith in him is superior. Consequently Paul can say: " The law was our custodian until Christ came, that we might be justified by faith. But now that faith has come, we are no longer under a custodian; for in Christ Jesus you are all sons of God, through faith." (Gal. 3:24-26.) The point is that Moses and Elijah have prepared the way for a greater teacher, and now that he has come, he is the authority, and we listen to him.

CHAPTER VI

The Biblical Faith of the Church

At the outset of our study we stated that many today regard the Bible as irrelevant to our time. We observed that several factors contribute to this prevailing attitude. The Bible is not always easy to read, it is sometimes hard to understand, some things found there are difficult to believe, and outmoded views as to what the Bible really is have contributed to the perplexity.

The historical approach we have adopted should go far to clarify some of the difficulties. We have observed how the Old Testament books came to be regarded as Scripture. Our examination of the claims the Bible makes as to prediction and fulfillment has provided evidence that extraordinary powers of second sight are not necessarily to be attributed to seers in ancient times. The Bible is not an unreasonable book, after all. In order to come to a still clearer perception of how to regard it, we need to be aware of certain thought forms and modes of expression that are characteristic of the Old Testament. Only as we achieve a more accurate realization of what the Bible really is can we avoid some of the pitfalls that beset us in our use of it.

Some Peculiarities of Hebrew Language and Thought

The forms of expression that prevail in the Old Testament are due in some measure to the characteristics of the language in which it was written. Except for a few portions, what we call

Biblical Hebrew was the language used. This was the tongue adopted by the tribes of Israel when they settled in Palestine. It was the West Semitic dialect spoken there by the Canaanites. It is essentially the same dialect that was spoken by their neighbors on the east and south, the Moabites and Edomites, and by the Phoenicians who lived to their west, along the Mediterranean coast. The Old Testament itself calls it " the lip of Canaan," and no doubt the parts of the Old Testament that were first written were set down in the Canaanite alphabet as well. The people who had been in Egypt probably had used the language of that country while there, but on their arrival in Canaan, they adopted the language of the land and made it their own.

Many centuries later, the North Semitic dialect of Syria known as Aramaic was recognized as more generally usable, and before the time of Christ, it had replaced " the lip of Canaan " and was the common spoken language of the Jews in New Testament times. Since the Aramaic alphabet was now more familiar, the books of the Old Testament were copied in that script. Consequently, what we call " Biblical Hebrew " is actually the Canaanite language written in the Aramaic alphabet.

The Semitic family of languages, to which Hebrew belongs, differs in significant respects from the Western tongues, derived through Greek and Latin, with which most of us are familiar. It will therefore be instructive for us to consider some of the peculiarities of the language of the Old Testament and to discover how these features may be of importance in helping us to regard these writings in proper perspective.

To begin with, Hebrew grammar has no way of indicating what one person may have told another except by quoting directly what was (or should have been) said. In English we can report a statement indirectly: " He said that he would come." Hebrew cannot do this. It must quote directly: " He said, ' I will come.' " The Old Testament does not say, indirectly, that the Lord made it known to Moses that he should go to Pharaoh and tell him to let the people of Israel go out of his land. Rather, the expression is direct: "And the Lord said to Moses, 'Go in, tell Pharaoh king of Egypt to let the people of Israel go out of his land.'" (Ex. 6:11.) Again, Jeremiah does not record that the Lord led him to the potter's house in order to teach him concerning his truth. Jeremiah puts it this way: "The word that came to Jeremiah from the Lord: 'Arise, and go down to the potter's house, and there I will let you hear my words.'" (Jer. 18:1-2.) Even an indefinite inner feeling is similarly reported, as when we read: "David said in his heart, 'I shall now perish one day by the hand of Saul; there is nothing better for me than that I should escape to the land of the Philistines.'" (I Sam. 27:1.)

This peculiarity of the language may account for the fact that divine inspiration is often expressed in terms of conversation. Lengthy speeches of the Lord are recorded in great detail, even on occasions when there was no one present to report what was said. The first chapter of Genesis relates the creation of the world as resulting from a series of statements by God which are given as quotations, though no man was there to hear them: "God said, 'Let there be light.'" "God said, 'Let there be a firmament in the midst of the waters, and let it separate the waters from the waters.'" "And God said, 'Let the earth bring forth living creatures according to their kinds: cattle and creeping things and beasts of the earth according to their kinds.' And it was so." (Gen. 1:3, 6, 24.)

The acts recorded as God's in the Old Testament are therefore called "the word of God." His act is his word. His purpose communicated to men is his word. The Ten Commandments are called in Hebrew "the Ten Words." The word of the Lord that came to the prophet was his inspiration, a sense that God had communicated his truth and called the prophet to action. Much futile debate has taken place over the question as to whether, when God spoke to the prophet, there was an audible sound or only an inner compulsion. If a tape recorder had been there, what would the tape have disclosed? The widespread perplexity among a good many Christians as to what is meant by God's word, or God's words, may be in some measure a result of this peculiarity of the Hebrew language.

A second peculiarity of Hebrew by which it differs from Western languages is in its system of verbs. It does not have " tenses," as does English, in which the past, present, and future are indicated. It has states, or conditions of the verb, in which there is an imperative, used in commands, and perfect and imperfect " tenses " that do not principally designate time at all. They indicate whether the action is completed, or is in process. It is as though the word " go " had really only two basic forms: " going " and " gone "; a process and a finished action.

A person might be *going* at the present moment, or he might be *going* next week, or he might have been *going* ten years ago. Similarly, one could have been *gone* last year, one could be *gone* at the present time, or one could be *gone* a month from now. In Hebrew the same form of the verb is used in each instance, no matter what is the time intended. The same word could be translated " he was speaking," " he is speaking," " he will be speaking," " let him speak," or even " he ought to speak." The intent as to time must be determined by the context, and sometimes this may be uncertain.

When a verb is translated, a time element is necessarily supplied, though lacking in Hebrew. English — and other European languages — forces us to do this, as the time of the action is a category determining the inflection of our verbs. By so doing, we inevitably limit or define the content of the original word, and there are some words which, when translated, no longer have the breadth of meaning that they do in Hebrew. A skillful translation is one that maintains the ambiguities of the original as frequently as possible, but no translation, however well done, can preserve them all.

An example of this is found in the explanation of the divine name " Yahweh " (" the Lord ") as described in the encounter of

Moses with God at the burning bush. In answer to Moses' question, "What is his name?" it is recorded that God said to Moses, "I am who I am" (Ex. 3:13-14). This assumes that the divine name is really the verb "to be" in the imperfect tense. But the Hebrew phrase means much more than "I am who I am." The Revised Standard Version recognizes this, and has a footnote that gives two alternates: "I am what I am," or "I will be what I will be." Yet these two suggestions by no means exhaust the possibilities. It could also mean, "I have been what I am," or "I will be what I have been," or "I am what I will be." There are other possibilities as well.

As a matter of fact, no translation into English is possible that will fully convey the flavor of the Hebrew phrase. What is suggested here is the timelessness and eternity of the Lord, and the unchangeableness and constancy of his nature. There is even the possibility suggested by modern scholars that what the name really signifies is God as Creator: "He who brings into being that which is." Perhaps the best solution is to do as the editors of the Revised Standard Version have done: to substitute for the divine Name the phrase "the Lord," and to discover from the theology of Scripture what he is really like — a God who created and sustains the world, who is motivated by steadfast love in his relations with men, who is perfectly consistent and eternal, indeed one who is the Father of his children.

Another example of how an English translation fails to represent the real meaning of the Hebrew is found in the familiar Twenty-third Psalm. Great numbers of people have learned by heart:

> The Lord is my shepherd, I shall not want;
>   he makes me lie down in green pastures.
> He leads me beside still waters;
>   he restores my soul.

The Hebrew verbs are a series of participles and imperfect tenses. In English, we shift the time element from the present to the future: "The Lord *is* my shepherd, I *shall* not want." But the Hebrew tense does not necessarily imply either time to the exclusion of the other. It suggests continuity without reference to time. If we could translate without bringing in the time factor, we should more accurately represent what is intended, though it would not then be good English sentence structure:

> The Lord, the one shepherding me,
> I lacking nothing;
> He, the one making me lie down in green pastures.
> He, the one leading me beside restful waters
> He, the restorer of my person.
>
> (Ps. 23:1-3.)

Such a rendering would suggest, as does the original, that in times past the Lord has shown himself to be this kind of shepherd, that he now acts in these ways, and that in future time he may be expected to continue to do so. In many other psalms the timelessness of the verbs has a significant value in relation to the theology they set forth.

A third peculiarity of the Hebrew language is the scarcity of adjectives. The language does have some adjectives: "large" and "small," "new" and "old," "good" and "bad," "righteous" and "wicked," and a few others. For the most part, however, adjectives are lacking. Their place is supplied by placing two nouns in close relationship, much like the possessive case in English, so that one qualifies the other. Hebrew cannot say "green grass," so it says "grass of greenness." For this reason we have become familiar with such phrases as "a man of valor," "a city of righteousness," "a God of steadfast love." Because we have become accustomed to this, it does not usually afford us difficulty. Yet there are occasions when the English equivalent may not suggest exactly what the original intended. Samuel is referred to as "a man of God." This is practically equivalent to the English "a godly man," which would mean, not that he had a quality of being which is

God's, but that he displayed characteristics and attitudes, motives, sympathies, and understandings which may be thought of as appropriate to God.

In Hebrew the term for "God" is always in the plural — "Gods." Much ingenuity has been expended to account for this. It has been supposed that this usage foreshadowed the Trinity; it has been suggested that it is a "plural of majesty," as though the person of God is too great to be contained in a singular form; it has been proposed that Deity associates with himself the members of a heavenly court — angels — so that "God" suggests heavenly authority. But the fact is that Israel adopted the Canaanite language, and, since the Canaanites were polytheists, believing in many gods, their word for deity occurred only in the plural form.

The Hebrew religious faith was so grounded in a belief in only one God that in adopting the plural form the writers used it with a singular verb, thereby evidencing their unique understanding of the unity of the divine Being, and their denial of the reality of other deities. Thus there is added significance in the affirmation of the people after Elijah's victory in his contest with the priests of Baal at Mt. Carmel: "The Lord, he is God; the Lord, he is God" (I Kings 18:39).

Furthermore, Hebrew is able to speak of groups of people as though they were a single individual. This usage is sometimes referred to as "corporate personality." When, in the days of Samuel, the Ark of God was captured by the Philistines and taken down to their coastal cities, we read that plague broke out among the people, and the Ark was removed from Ashdod to Gath. Here again there was affliction, so the Ark was moved again to Ekron. The grammatical phrase in Hebrew would most accurately be translated thus: "The people of Ekron cried out, 'They have brought around to me the ark of the God of Israel to slay me and my people!'" (I Sam. 5:10.)

Many of the psalms express the lament or yearning of an individual as though a particular worshiper were speaking. Yet some of these are, without doubt, not prayers of individual persons but of the personified community. The individuals who comprise the congregation identify themselves with one another so that they become one, and speak as a single person. In Ps. 129:3 it is Israel who says,

> The plowers plowed upon my back;
> they made long their furrows.

In Ps. 89:39-40 it is the nation to which reference is made:

> Thou hast renounced the covenant with thy servant;
> thou hast defiled his crown in the dust.
> Thou hast breached all his walls;
> thou hast laid his strongholds in ruins.

These are obvious examples, but we may well ask whether it is an individual worshiper or the corporate community that speaks in many other psalms, including prayers of thanksgiving, petition, confession, and praise, in which the pronouns and verbs are singular.

It is a common procedure for the prophets to refer to Israel as " Jacob," the alternate name of their reputed ancestor, and to address their messages as to a single personification. The same is true of the designations of the several tribes that made up the nation. It is probable that the names of some tribes were geographical in origin, rather than personal. It seems from its usage that Ephraim was first the name for a part of the land in the north, and that " Ephraimites " were properly inhabitants of that region. Likewise, the designation " Benjamites," which means " sons of the south," may be used in the same way as that in which Job is called " the greatest of all the people of the east " (Hebrew: " sons of the east ") (Job 1:3). Nevertheless, Jeremiah represents the Lord as saying,

> . . . I am a father to Israel,
> and Ephraim is my first-born.
> (Jer. 31:9.)

The famous blessing of Jacob upon his twelve sons (Gen. 49:2-27) refers to each of them as individuals, though many of the descriptions are tribal in reference, and v. 28 explains: " All these are the twelve tribes of Israel." So, also, have we already seen that the Servant of the Lord, where the words are used in the singular, has at least in some cases a collective reference to the nation. (Isa. 41:8-10; 42:18-25; 43:10; 44:1-5; etc.) Probably the doctrine of the Servant of the Lord can best be understood by taking into account the idea of corporate personality.

Finally, we may note that the Hebrew mind ordinarily takes no account of secondary causation. Whatever occurs is directly the act of God. If there is famine, drought, blight, or pestilence, this is because the Lord directly caused it. (Amos 4:6-10.) Hannah had no children because " the Lord had closed her womb " (I Sam. 1:6). She prayed for a child, and " the Lord remembered her; and in due time Hannah conceived and bore a son " (I Sam. 1:19-20). Biblical poetry frequently reflects this immediacy in God's working.

> The Lord kills and brings to life;
>   he brings down to Sheol and raises up.
> The Lord makes poor and makes rich;
>   he brings low, he also exalts.
>
>   (I Sam. 2:6-7.)

We read that Moses broke the two tables on which God had written ten commandments, when he found the people had made a golden calf, and later returned to Sinai to replace them. It is stated that " the Lord said to Moses, ' Cut two tables of stone like the first; and I will write upon the tables the words that were on the first tables, which you broke ' " (Ex. 34:1). Later in the same chapter, after giving him further instructions, " the Lord said to Moses, ' Write these words; in accordance with these words I have made a covenant with you and with Israel.' And he was there with the Lord forty days and forty nights; he neither ate bread nor drank water. And he wrote upon the tables the words of the covenant, the ten commandments." (Ex. 34:27-28.) To the Hebrew mind these are two ways of saying the same thing. God writes; Moses writes. When a prophet speaks, God speaks. If there is a military victory, God wins the battle for them. If they do not win, God smites his people.

The reader of the Bible must therefore be aware that certain forms of phrase are characteristic of the language in which it is written, and that various modes of expression were habitually used in Biblical times. Our understanding of the meaning is conditioned by these considerations. Whether words are to be taken by us at face value, or whether they are subject to interpretation in the light of such elements, is something that must always be kept in mind. An unduly literal adherence to the phraseology may lead us astray in our discovery of what was meant by the authors. An uncritical attitude on our part simply will not be adequate.

CONTINUING FULFILLMENT OF THE LAW AND THE PROPHETS

If we accept the contention that the Law and the Prophets are fulfilled in the life and work of Jesus as the Christ, and if they are indeed the custodian to bring us to him, the question then arises: Is it important to the twentieth-century Christian to try to make any further use of them? If Christ is our teacher, and we are to listen to him, why need we concern ourselves further with the earlier stages? Are we not brought back directly to the matter of their relevance to us today?

Paul states unequivocally his contention that we are justified in the sight of God not by works of the law but by faith in Christ (Rom. 5:1). This means recognition of the purport of his life and work, and active response to it. It means participation in the kind of life to which this faith obligates us. Paul therefore goes on to say that we are not under law but under grace (Rom. 6:14). To many this seems to say that consequently we may disregard the law entirely. What significance has it for us?

Yet the meaning of the grace of the gospel can be appreciated only against the background of what preceded it. Paul was speaking primarily of the "works of the law" (Gal. 2:16) by which no one is justified in God's sight. As we have seen, although Jesus accepted the law, he did not consider scrupulous observance of minute regulations after the manner of the Pharisees as either valuable or necessary. On the other hand, the Old Testament law is not simply to be equated with legislation and regulation. It is much more than that. To reduce it to a series of formalities to be observed is to miss its true significance. The modern Christian is prone to impose upon the word "law" a connotation of legal enactment. Actually, the Hebrew word is "torah," a term derived from a root meaning "to instruct" or "to direct." Law is properly "instruction" or "direction," an indication as to the way those who were under the covenant should order their thinking and their national life.

"The law was given through Moses," says the New Testament; "grace and truth came through Jesus Christ." (John 1:17.) Just what was the law given through Moses? The elaborate civil, social, and religious regulations that comprise much of the Pentateuch are not the entire content of the Torah. Fundamental was the sense of divine vocation: "For you are a people holy to the Lord your God; the Lord your God has chosen you to be a people for his own possession, out of all the peoples that are on the face of the earth" (Deut. 7:6). The purpose of the law was to set forth a national responsibility that the people might come to understand what it means to live in the light of the favor of God, and to exhibit a community life in accordance with that favor.

The Pentateuch is not alone comprised of the regulations and enactments to which Paul referred. Instruction is by example as well as by precept. Here are accounts of the patriarchal ancestors of the people, in which success and failure are both narrated, in which noble insights and dismal shortcomings are fully described, in order to indicate direction for living. Here are great traditions of divine guidance in the early history of the people. Especially in the book of Deuteronomy the emphasis is ethical rather than material, directed toward right attitudes rather than toward ritualistic observances. There is a timeless element in the statement which has become the central affirmation of Judaism: "Hear, O Israel: The Lord our God is one Lord; and you shall love the Lord your God with all your heart, and with all your soul, and with all your might." (Deut. 6:4-5.) Such a principle is in no way outmoded by a gospel of the grace of God. Jesus himself quoted these words when asked what one should do to inherit eternal life, and joined with them another passage from the law, "You shall love your neighbor as yourself" (Lev. 19:18), asserting that "on these two commandments depend all the law and the prophets" (Matt. 22:35-40; Mark 12:28-34; Luke 10:25-28). Love toward God and neighbor is not the exclusive teaching of the New Testament; it is repeatedly enjoined in the Law: "What does the Lord your God require of you, but to fear the Lord your God, to walk in all his ways, to love him, to serve the Lord your God with all your heart and with all your soul, and to keep the commandments and statutes of the Lord, which I command you this day for your good?" (Deut. 10:12-13.) Fathers are called upon to make known to their children, and to their children's children through the generations, the great tradition of God's covenant with them.

These are important truths, valuable in every age. How can we say that they are outmoded? The New Testament fulfills them in the sense of corroboration, amplification, repetition, and re-evaluation. In Christ they come to even deeper meaning. By no means are they abolished by grace! This would be false both to the method of Jesus and to his message. There should be continuing fulfillment of such values through Christian life and experience, not by contrasting law with gospel, but by recognizing the continuity of one in the other.

A similar continuity may be discerned in the books of the prophets. The outlook of the prophets, as has been pointed out, was chiefly toward their own age; but in adopting this outlook, they also took into consideration both the past and the future.

Just as the present had grown out of the past, so the future would derive in considerable measure from the present. The prophets therefore looked both backward and forward, in order to speak to the present. Because their message was grounded in the realities of human experience, they speak also to our day, though we must reject the once prevalent but mistaken notion that they envisioned our times and described them in coded expressions now perceived to have a meaning.

Part of our problem stems from the way the word "prophet" is commonly used. The English word is ordinarily equated with prediction, and with prediction only. We speak of "weather prophets," by which we mean those who profess to tell what kind of weather is in store in the future; we mention "political prophets," meaning those who forecast the future complexion of the political scene; "economic prophets" are those who look to the future of the economic system. We coin such phrases as "prophets of doom," or "prophets of a better day," and similar expressions. All of these presuppose that a prophet is primarily a foreteller of the future.

An apparent grammatical justification for this lies in the word itself. "Prophet" is from two Greek words, "to speak" and "before." It is ordinarily supposed that this means "to speak before the event." But this is a superficial view, receiving support in turn from the popular assumption and usage just mentioned. Actually, the element "before" refers not so much to time as to position: the prophet is "in front," not that he is previous to the event, but that he is in the forefront with respect to the one for whom he speaks. The prophet is "before" in location as respects his source of inspiration: he stands "in front" of God to proclaim the divine purpose. He is a spokesman.

In his experience at the burning bush, Moses protests that he is not eloquent. The Lord is represented as directing his attention to his brother Aaron, who can speak well. "He shall speak for you to the people; and he shall be a mouth for you, and you shall be to him as God." (Ex. 4:16.) This is repeated in a later chapter: "See, I make you as God to Pharaoh; and Aaron your brother shall be your prophet." (Ex. 7:1.) Aaron is "before" Moses, as his spokesman, his "prophet." This is the correct Old Testament usage of the word and is basic to our understanding of the role of the prophet in Israel.

That this interpretation is correct is attested by the use of the word in designating the books of the prophets. The "Former Prophets" are the books of Joshua, Judges, Samuel, and Kings. They contain accounts of the conquest of Palestine under Joshua and his successors, the division of the land among the tribes, and the deeds of charismatic leaders who vindicated the religion of Israel by military victories. They further tell of the exploits of Saul and David, the magnificent reign of Solomon, the division of the kingdom into two, and the vicissitudes of Israel and Judah until their conquest by Assyria and Babylonia. We call such books history. But they are history with an interpretation. Judgment is passed on the various participants in the history. Their acts are characterized as good or bad, as righteous or unrighteous, as pleasing in the sight of the Lord or displeasing. These judgments are evaluations on the part of the historians. By being classified as "former prophets," these books are defined as prophecy. Yet they relate what happened in the past, critically estimated in the light of Israel's faith. They are not descriptions of days to come. Nevertheless, they are properly prophetic in tone and purpose, and we should note this fact in defining the word "prophet."

When the books of the prophets are mentioned, the average churchman thinks of what are called the Major and the Minor Prophets. These are the "Latter Prophets" of the second part of the Hebrew Bible, but it will be recalled that Daniel was not part of this canon at the time of its formation. When the Hebrew books were translated into Greek, they were rearranged in order according to types of literature, and the apocalyptic book of Daniel was included here. From the later Latin Bible, translated in turn from the Greek, come the designations "major" and "minor" as applied to the prophetic books. The Latin words of course refer to size and not to importance. They simply mean " larger " and " smaller " prophets, not ones of greater or of less significance.

As a matter of fact, the New Testament refers to David as a prophet, and even to Abraham. This inclusive use of the word is itself instructive. The term is not limited in its use to the dynamic leaders whose messages are preserved in writing, or even to others like Nathan, Ahijah, Elijah, Micaiah, and Iddo, who, if they did write, have left nothing for us. All of them were men of real purpose, remembered for their zeal in rebuking religious carelessness, selfish and thoughtless rulers, and the social evils of their time, and tireless in their efforts to proclaim, extend, and purify the worship of the one true God. Their view ranged from events of past generations to hopes of the future. They described actual conditions, and portrayed ideal ones. Most of all, they were the critics of their own day, forever urging upon their contemporaries the demands of the ancient covenant, and speaking in the name and on behalf of the God of their fathers.

To make the reading of the prophets relevant to the twentieth century, misconceptions concerning them must be cleared away; they must be read for what they are. Then they will be perceived as speaking *to* our day rather than *about* it. Their significance for us is not that they described our times, but that as precursors of the Christian gospel they announced timeless truths of religious faith. No wonder Jesus could say of love toward God and love toward neighbor, " On these two depend all the law and the prophets."

Because the truths they announced are constant, there is still the prospect of continuing fulfillment from generation to generation. Men are ever in need of being led to the threshold of the Christian gospel. Therefore the relevance of the law and the prophets is that they deepen and enhance appreciation of Christian truth. They are the backdrop against which it is possible to observe more accurately the uniqueness of the Christian faith and life; but they are also part of that experience, and come into their own when the Christian way of life is most completely followed.

When that happens, once more they find fulfillment. The need of every generation is for continuing fulfillment of both the law and the prophets.

THE BIBLE AS THE WORD OF GOD

The faith of the church includes, among other elements, the affirmation that the Bible is the Word of God. This has meant different things to different people. To some it has meant that whatever is written in the Bible is of absolute authority for all generations, and that what was once authoritative will always be so. For others it has meant that the Bible "contains" the word of God, and the reader must be in position to determine what may be and what may not be authoritative for a given generation. For still others the phrase connotes that in Scripture, God has something to say to mankind, and that the Bible as a whole is a divine word, though particular parts may be subject to more selective examination. We do well to examine the possibilities here and to discover, as far as we may, what significance these ideas may have for our time.

We have said that the acts recorded as God's in the Old Testament are called the "word of God." We need to define more exactly both the Hebrew and the English use of the term "word." What is meant by the familiar line, "Thy word is a lamp to my feet and a light to my path"? (Ps. 119:105.) Is it proper to apply this to the Bible as a whole? The average churchman is inclined to do so. But when the psalm was written, how much of the Bible existed? Possibly the Pentateuch had come into its present form, and perhaps some of the books of the prophets had taken shape, but the third section of the Old Testament, the Writings, had not yet been compiled, and certainly none of the New Testament had yet appeared. What did the psalmist have in mind? Did he speak of the five books of Moses?

Consider the following examples: The Book of Hosea begins with the phrase, "The word of the Lord that came to Hosea." The Book of Joel begins, "The word of the Lord that came to

Joel." Isaiah 2:1 reads, " The word which Isaiah the son of Amoz saw concerning Judah and Jerusalem." Surely these references are not to a book, or a collection of books, but to something else. To equate the idea of " word " with a written book is obviously inadequate.

Each of the foregoing evidently refers to prophetic inspiration. The message of the prophet is taken to mean, not that the prophet speaks his own ideas, but that he utters what has been divinely implanted in him. Jeremiah repeatedly introduces his oracles with the phrase, " Thus says the Lord," or, " Then the Lord said to me." " When the Lord first spoke through Hosea " (Hos. 1:2) indicates that the words are Hosea's, but that he understands that he is expressing the Lord's purpose as he speaks. There is a distinction between the *words* and the *word*.

When Pentecost had come, we read that Peter and John " spoke the word of God with boldness " (Acts 4:31). Surely this does not refer to a book, but rather to the preaching of the gospel. Later we read that " the word of God increased; and the number of the disciples multiplied greatly in Jerusalem " (Acts 6:7). We are evidently to understand that as the news of the gospel became more widespread and effective, the augmentation of the number of believers marked the increase of the word of God. The author of The Letter to the Hebrews begins his epistle by saying: " In many and various ways God spoke of old to our fathers by the prophets; but in these last days he has spoken to us by a Son." Here is a reference to Jesus as the Word, a concept that finds fuller expression in the opening chapter of the Gospel of John: " In the beginning was the Word, and the Word was with God, and the Word was God. . . . And the Word became flesh and dwelt among us, full of grace and truth." (John 1:1, 14.)

The Biblical concept of word is therefore much wider than an idea applicable only to a book. *Word is a means of communication.* " The word " is an expression indicating that the Lord has made something known to man. In human usage, words are instruments by which men arouse in others concepts similar to those which are their own. By words we produce ideas in other minds like those which are in ours. So in the Biblical usage, God is said to communicate ideas to men, and this is conceived as being by means of a word. The communication may be in the mind of the prophet, it may be by outward event, it may be the teaching of the gospel, it may be through Christ as incarnate Word. However that communication takes place, it is understood to mean that men have received fresh insight into God's nature, purpose, and truth.

When we say that the Book is God's word, this is in part what we mean. The written words, when properly perceived and evaluated, are understood to create within the reader a realization of God's way, purpose, or will that is new and different. At this point the Bible has acted as God's word.

Furthermore, in Biblical usage word is not only a means of communication, it is also *the content of what is revealed*. Word not only is the means of arousing a knowledge of truth, but is itself the truth. Jesus applied it to the law when he accused the Pharisees of " making void the word of God through your tradition which you hand on " (Mark 7:13). On another occasion when he said, " Blessed rather are those who hear the word of God and keep it " (Luke 11:28), he was evidently referring to God's revealed will, his whole plan and purpose for mankind. This general sense as being the content of revealed truth is what was intended by Paul when he wrote: " It is not as though the word of God had failed. For not all who are descended from Israel belong to Israel, and not all are children of Abraham because they are his descendants " (Rom. 9:6-7). In this same sense he wrote concerning his ministry, " which was given to me for you, to make the word of God fully known, the mystery hidden for ages and generations but now made manifest to his saints " (Col. 1:25-26).

The preaching of Jesus is called the word of God: " While the people pressed upon him to hear the word of God, he was standing by the lake of Gennesaret." (Luke 5:1.) In recording the prayer of Jesus for his church, John includes the following: "I have manifested thy name to the men whom thou gavest me out of the world; thine they were, and thou gavest them to me, and they have kept thy word." (John 17:6.) The reference seems to be to his own teaching. We have already indicated that in the preaching of the apostles, their message concerning Jesus was preaching the word.

Still further, word is not only communication, not only content, but *motivating power*. The book of Hebrews states: "For the word of God is living and active, sharper than any two-edged sword, piercing to the division of soul and spirit, of joints and marrow, and discerning the thoughts and intentions of the heart." (Heb. 4:12.) Paul writes that "the word of the cross is folly to those who are perishing, but to us who are being saved it is the power of God" (I Cor. 1:18). He then points out that in preaching Christ crucified, his speech and message "were not in plausible words of wisdom, but in demonstration of the Spirit and power, that your faith might not rest in the wisdom of men but in the power of God" (I Cor. 2:4-5).

Through his word, God empowers those who heed it to move toward the goals it indicates. The call of God is also an impelling force: those who are filled with the word are imbued with the means of achievement. To respond to the word is to work toward its realization. *Word is communication, content, and power.*

On the basis of these premises, let us examine the assertion that the Bible is the Word of God. The Book is one of the means by which God seeks to communicate with men. It is a continuing means by which the substance of divine truth is imparted to men. The content of Scripture, however familiar, retains a capacity for producing in the reader new insights, new depths of comprehension, new attitudes toward problems of time and eternity. A passage long known may shine forth with fresh brilliance and significance. At that point the Bible has spoken. It has become God's word. By so doing, it has exhibited itself as a means of revelation, an instrument of divine purpose.

There are two ways of expressing this. One is to say that the Bible *is* the Word of God. Another is to say that the Bible *contains* the word of God. Both statements are true. The first is true in that it describes what happens when a person gains fresh insight from perceiving what is for him new truth. The second is true in that not every passage of Scripture speaks to one with equal effect, but there are passages which, when encountered in the right setting, communicate with new authority. Truth is contained in the Book.

The Word of God and the Words of Men

A significant product of modern Biblical study lies in the realization that the Bible also consists of the words of men. Just as " the Lord spoke through Hosea," so he spoke also through Moses and Elijah, Matthew and Luke, Peter and Paul. Each of these was a person in his own right, and what he said was addressed to a particular historic situation. None of them, in all probability, thought of himself as an author of Holy Scripture. Moses was intent on welding his people into a nation, in common allegiance to the one true God. The prophets were directly concerned with events and circumstances in their own times. They wanted their hearers to believe and to act in accordance with that belief. Paul wrote his letters to Christians whom he knew or with whom he had made contact. He addressed himself directly to questions that his friends in Corinth had asked, to the situation as he understood it, and to the needs he felt to be urgent under prevailing conditions.

It is therefore apparent that not all of Scripture is on the same level so far as we are concerned, nor is every part of equal importance to us. Some teachings are of universal significance, important for every age, under whatever conditions may prevail. Other parts are of quite local and temporary value. Paul writes to Timothy reminding him of the permanent values in the gospel, and urging faithfulness in its proclamation. In the same letter he asks Timothy to bring the cloak that he had left at Troas, sends news as to the whereabouts of mutual friends, and asks that his greetings be conveyed to certain persons he names (II Tim., chs. 1; 2; 4). To the Corinthians he wrote answers to specific questions they had put to him, and in at least one case prefaced his advice by cautioning, "I have no command of the Lord, but I give my opinion as one who by the Lord's mercy is trustworthy" (I Cor. 7:25). It would be hard to claim for this advice divine authority, since the apostle indicates that it is only his best judgment. So the Bible contains not only the word of God but also the words of men. Can we distinguish one from the other? To what extent is it necessary to do so?

The fact is that every part of Scripture is found in a particular framework or setting. The more accurately we perceive the setting, the better we shall be able to separate what is local and temporary from what is general and timeless. We should make an effort to distinguish the picture from the frame. When we have done so, we are in position to determine whether there is a word from God, and what that word may be. In a large number of instances, the particular expression of the prophet, apostle, or Gospel writer is so phrased because of certain basic understandings that lie behind it. Particular and local application is made of some more general principle. If we can read behind the lines, discovering *why* the human words took this form, we may be able to discern a more general truth, and the word of God will be found there rather than in the way it happens to be expressed. In fact, the same basic truth may lie behind teachings that appear to be directly opposite to one another.

Our purpose in the study of the Bible should be to become better informed as to what it teaches. Men have quoted the Bible to support all kinds of opinions which are assuredly not in conformity with the tenor of Christian faith and action. It is proverbial that the devil can quote Scripture for his purpose. Only by care in the use of a historical approach can we be certain as to the real message that the Bible has.

An example of this might be the question, Does Scripture teach that God wishes his people to have a temple? In the book of Exodus, the emphasis is on a movable shrine, the Tabernacle. In Samuel's time, the symbol of worship was the Ark of the Covenant, kept in an apparently permanent building in Shiloh. Solomon undertook to build a royal shrine in Jerusalem, the work being done by craftsmen from Tyre. Clearly, The First Book of the Kings teaches that it is God's will that the Temple be built. But by the time of the prophets of the eighth and seventh centuries B.C., the Temple services were not so regarded. One after another of the prophets denounces the ritual of Temple worship, claiming it not to be what the Lord desires, and holding that people have let the building and its rites obscure true religion. Jeremiah called for his hearers to amend their ways, asserting that their trust in the Temple was of no avail. He called the shrine " a den of robbers " and announced that it would be destroyed, as was Shiloh (Jer., ch. 7). Of the Ark of the Covenant he said, " It shall not come to mind, or be remembered, or missed; it shall not be made again " (ch. 3:16). Nebuchadrezzar came, the Temple was destroyed, and Jeremiah announced that in a far country true worship of God would replace the false worship of the Temple.

Yet, in that distant land, far from reminders of the faith of their fathers, people in great measure became careless and forgetful of their heritage. So Ezekiel preached the eventuality of a return to their homeland and announced that the Temple must be rebuilt. He viewed the building and its courts as an essential part of religion in the restored community. When the first returning representatives of the nation arrived, they looked with dismay upon the ruins. The task of reconstruction seemed forbidding. For sixteen years no temple was started; then Haggai and Zechariah announced the Lord's will that his house should be rebuilt, and under Zerubbabel and Joshua the task was completed. With the resumption of ritual, it became apparent again that rites were replacing righteousness, and prophetic denunciation of this fact appears in the last ten chapters of Isaiah, and in The Book of Malachi.

The time eventually came when Jesus himself was incensed by the perversion of the Temple into mere formality. He cast out the money-changers and overturned their tables and the seats of those who sold pigeons for the sacrifices. He quoted Jeremiah's phrase about the "den of robbers." On another occasion, when his disciples were admiring the splendor of the buildings, he said: "There will not be left here one stone upon another, that will not be thrown down." This came about when Titus, the Roman emperor, conquered Jerusalem in A.D. 70, and took some of the equipment of the shrine triumphantly to Rome. Since that time, there has been no temple.

The question is, Does Scripture say that we should or should not have a temple? The answer must be that it says both. Some passages say that it should be built as the center of worship. Other passages say that it should not continue, for it is an obstruction to true worship. Which is the teaching of Scripture?

The teaching of Scripture is basically that any such building is secondary to the worshipers who would use it. The Bible points to human values first. If a particular building will help, by all means make a place for it; if the building is a hindrance to the more important things of the spirit, by all means do away with it. Sincerity in worship, accompanied by righteousness of life, was what every prophet pronounced to be the Lord's demand. The building itself is but incidental.

Thus, if we ask what is the word of God in Scripture, we must search behind the incidents of the moment to discern the eternal principles upon which the temporal teaching is based. These eternal principles, in every instance, are the true word of God.

The Church as the New Israel

As the number of adherents to the Christian faith multiplied in the lands beyond the borders of Israel, the number of those who had not come up through the traditions of Judaism increased. Theirs was a Gentile background, stemming from the Greek and Roman cultures. It was therefore incumbent upon the church to reexamine its understanding of their relation to the Palestinian heritage. It was understood that the inclusiveness of faith in Christ knew no barrier of race or nationality. How, then, should the ancient tradition of God's promises to Abraham and his descendants be regarded as respecting Gentile Christians? The church understood Jesus to be the culmination of the Old Testament promises, and his message to be the continuation and consummation of the teaching through the generations past. In the New Testament we sense a growing conviction that those who came from other backgrounds were fully entitled to participate in the common tradition. This finds expression in the idea of the church as the New Israel, with whom God has made the new covenant to succeed the old. Paul calls it " the Israel of God " (Gal. 6:16).

The commonly accepted view had been that those who were truly Israel were so by biological descent, and by national and cultural inheritance. The Pharisees and Sadducees had prided themselves that they could trace their descent from Abraham. John the Baptist had early challenged this, when he is reported to have chided them: " Bear fruit that befits repentence, and do not presume to say to yourselves, 'We have Abraham as our father'; for I tell you, God is able from these stones to raise up children to Abraham." (Matt. 3:8-9.) To put this in other words, John told them that physical descent was without special significance, unless a spirit of contrition brought about a reversal of attitude and life; even in that case such descent would be decidedly secondary if God could bring dead stones into the same inheritance.

A different approach is made in the teaching of Paul. Gentiles who have accepted the Way of Christ are, as it were, adopted into the nation, and become legal descendants of the patriarchal ancestor. To the Galatians he writes most significantly: " For as many of you as were baptized into Christ have put on Christ. There is neither Jew nor Greek, there is neither slave nor free, there is neither male nor female; for you are all one in Christ

Jesus. And if you are Christ's, then you are Abraham's offspring, heirs according to promise." (Gal. 3:27-29.) This is the position that is taken up by other New Testament writers and gives rise to the designation of followers of Christ as the Israel of God.

The Israel of God is in contrast to what may be called Israel after the flesh. The New Israel is a community of faith, based upon a qualitative relationship with God resulting from a realization of what God has done for man through Christ's work. There is a corporate hope that binds its members together, just as there was understood to be a corporate covenant with the nation of old. It involves both promise and hope. The realization and actuality through Christian experience of some of the yearnings of prophetic voices in the past give rise to hope for consummation and completion of these and others in the future. Paul understands that the church has come into being by God's election to which man's faith responds. Such faith knows no limit of natural descent. He states it thus to the Romans: "That is why it depends on faith, in order that the promise may rest on grace and be guaranteed to all his descendants — not only to the adherents of the law but also to those who share the faith of Abraham, for he is the father of us all, as it is written, 'I have made you the father of many nations.'" (Rom. 4:16-17.) Paul thus defends here, and in others of his letters, the full participation of non-Jews in the implications of the ancient promises to Israel.

The faith to which he refers is of course faith in Jesus as the Christ, who opened a new conception and comprehension of the will of God, evidenced by his own death to make it possible. Those who accept this principle and make it effective for themselves by participating actively in whatever it implies become the church, which thereby is seen as a community living in the present and looking toward the future. The Israel of God relies on further promises of the ultimate full achievement of the true Kingdom of God, and so looks toward a coming salvation completely brought to perfection, rather than back toward a past deliverance. It understands itself as striving for a goal, rather than relying on former evidences of accomplishment. It is represented as the New Israel, or, even more, as the true Israel.

In consequence, it places upon the Christian community the obligation for continuing fulfillment, in days still ahead of us, of promises seen to be inherent in the revelation of past and present. It is not sufficient to claim that Old Testament expectations, symbols, and representations have been or are being fulfilled by the coming of Christ and the establishment of the church. Many promises and expectations still are short of finality. The faith of the church is that *their completion must yet come*. This faith is of the same kind that we noted in the prophets. We observed that these men did not so much predict what was going to happen as give expression to what *must* happen if God is truly sovereign. Our anticipation must be the same.

If the church may be represented as the New Israel, it is then apparent how other images and figures connected with the ancient life of the nation came to be applied symbolically to the church. James speaks of Christians as inheriting the Kingdom: " Has not God chosen those who are poor in the world to be rich in faith and heirs of the kingdom which he has promised to those who love him? " (James 2:5.) Similarly, " therefore let us be grateful for receiving a kingdom that cannot be shaken " (Heb. 12:28). Christ is King and, according to Paul, " much more will those who receive the abundance of grace and the free gift of righteousness reign in life through the one man Jesus Christ " (Rom. 5:17). The New Israel is God's new Kingdom.

Since a temple characterized the worship of the Old Israel, so the New Israel has its temple. " What agreement has the temple of God with idols? For we are the temple of the living God." (II Cor. 6:16.) This temple is a structure, built upon foundations, but its stones *grow,* for it is a living building. "You are fellow citizens with the saints and members of the household of God, built upon the foundation of the apostles and prophets, Christ Jesus himself being the cornerstone, in whom the whole structure is joined together and grows into a holy temple in the Lord; in whom you also are built into it for a dwelling place of God in the Spirit." (Eph. 2:19-22.) Thus the church is the New Israel, its members grow into a temple, Christ is the High Priest, who offered himself also as sacrifice; therefore at the altar "let us continually offer up a sacrifice of praise to God, that is, the fruit of lips that acknowledge his name" (Heb. 13:15). This is continuing fulfillment in its true sense. Paul uses a similar figure: "I appeal to you therefore, brethren, by the mercies of God, to present your bodies as a living sacrifice, holy and acceptable to God, which is your spiritual worship." (Rom. 12:1.)

The church is also considered the household of God (Heb. 3:2-6; I Peter 4:17), in which God is the father and the members are brothers (I Cor. 6:6; I John 3:10-17; I Peter 2:17). As members of the household, they are figuratively members of the body of Christ, who is himself the head (Eph. 4:15; Col. 1:18). The health of the entire body depends upon the soundness of each of the members. This indicates a concern of each Christian for his fellows, to the end that the whole may grow in strength and well-being.

The concept of prediction and fulfillment is thus seen to be a continuing process, not a finished phenomenon. Our task at the outset of our study was to become informed as to what was meant by expressions that claimed achievement of previous expectation in events in the New Testament story. By discovering that fulfillment leads eventually to complete consummation, we learn that the days are yet to come when the gospel will be realized in its fullness, when the brotherhood which we have described becomes truly effective for every individual, when outward fact will correspond with the hope expressed "that at the name of Jesus every knee should bow, in heaven and on earth and under the earth, and every tongue confess that Jesus Christ is Lord, to the glory of God the Father" (Phil. 2:10-11). That will be the day when swords will at last be beaten into plowshares and spears into pruning-hooks. The fulfillment of the final goal lies yet ahead. Our responsibility as followers of Christ is to heed the religious and social implications, not only of the law and the prophets, but also of the Christian faith. Let us strive to follow the injunction of the apostle: " Bear one another's burdens, and so fulfil the law of Christ." (Gal. 6:2.)

Subject Index

Aaron, 110, 134
Abraham, 31, 145
Adjectives, scarcity of, 127
Adventists, 14
Ahaz, 23, 24, 75
Ahijah, 76
Alexander the Great, 32
Allusion, 94
Amaziah, 83
Amos, 83
Antioch of Pisidia, 34
Apocrypha, 17, 47, 60
Aquila, 60
Aramaic, 123
Assumption of Moses, 47
Authority of the Bible, 11, 17

Baruch, 52
Bethlehem, 22, 25, 26
Bible, 47
Biblical Hebrew, 123
Branch, 27

Caesar Augustus, 81
Canon of Scripture, 46, 47, 60
Church, 144, 148

Cleopatra's Needles, 81
Conditional predictions, 77
Conference at Jerusalem, 30
Constantine, 80
Continuing fulfillment, 131, 147
Corban, 42
Cornerstone, 37, 63
Corporate personality, 115, 128
Council of Jamnia, 60
Covenant, 50, 117
Cyprian, 36

Daniel, 59, 103
Day of the Lord, 33, 86, 100
Delphi, 68
Den of robbers, 44, 144
Deuteronomy, 50
Divination, 68, 71

Ecclesiasticus, 47, 58
End of the age, 85, 92, 93
Enoch, Book of, 47, 104
Entry into Jerusalem, 28
Exclusiveness, 88
Ezra, 55, 88

False prophets, 50, 71, 72, 73, 108
Feast of Booths, 55
Finger of God, 10
Flight into Egypt, 20
Former Prophets, 56, 135
Fulfilled predictions, 74
Fulfillment, 12, 13, 66, 94, 103, 119

God, 128
Gospels' use of the Old Testament, 19
Great commandment, 54, 133
Great Commission, 91
Great Hallel, 63

Hagar, 24
Haggai, 54, 143
Hanamel, 28
Hananiah, 75
Hebrew language, 122
Hebrew tenses, 125
Hebrews, The Letter to the, 109, 111
Heliopolis, 80
Herod, 20, 21
Hezekiah, 76
Historical approach to the Bible, 11, 17, 63, 65, 122, 141
Holiness Code, 54
Huldah, 49

Immanuel, 23, 75
Indirect discourse, 123
Individual responsibility, 50
Ishmael, 24

Jamnia, Council of, 60
Jehoiachin, 82
Jehoiakim, 52, 82
Jehoshaphat, 87
Jeroboam, 74, 78, 83
Jesus' use of the Old Testament, 38, 45
John the Baptist, 26, 27
Jonah, 43, 89
Josiah, 49, 53, 78
Judas, 28
Judgment, 86, 87

Kingdom of God, 32, 64, 101

Last Supper, 63, 113, 118
Latter Prophets, 56, 135
Law, 53

Maccabees, Books of the, 58, 59
Melchizedek, 112
Messiah, 96, 97
Micaiah, 72
Millenarians, 14
Mixed marriages, 88
Money changers, 44
Moses, 50, 51, 53, 120, 134
Moses, five books of, 54

Nationalism, 91
Nazareth, 27, 39, 40
Nebuchadrezzar, 79
New Covenant, 117
New Israel, 144, 147

Obelisks, 80
Oral tradition, 38

Parables, 41, 43
Pashhur, 84
Passover, 50
Pentecost, 33, 138
Pharisees, 32, 145
Philip, 116
Pilate, 33
Potter's field, 28
Predictive prophecy, 74, 82
Priest, 109
Priesthood, 109
Promises to Abraham, 31, 89
Prophet, 106, 108, 134
Prophets as Scripture, 56

Queen of Sheba, 44

Rachel's tomb, 22
Resurrection, 92
Revelation of God, 53
Revised Standard Version, 126
Roman converts, 31
Ruth, 89

Sacred lot, 69
Sacrifice, 96, 109, 110
Sadducees, 32, 145
Salvation, 86
Samaritans, 56
Saul, 78
Secondary causation, 130
Seer, 78
Sennacherib, 75
Septuagint, 60
Servant of the Lord, 90, 113
Shebna, 84
Shepherd, 98

Signs, 43, 69
Slaughter of the innocents, 21
Solomon, 44, 76
Son of Man, 96, 102
Spirituality of God, 50
Stone rejected by the builders, 37, 63
Synagogue, 55

Tabernacle, 110
Temple, 49, 51, 89, 143
Tenses, Hebrew, 125
Testimonies, 35, 36, 63
Thirty pieces of silver, 28, 37
Transfiguration, 120
Treasury, 28
Tyre, 79

Unity of God, 50
Universalism, 91
Unfulfilled predictions, 79
Unleavened bread, 49
Urim and Thummim, 69

Virgin, 23, 25

Wisdom of God, 48
Wisdom of Solomon, 47
Word of God, 137
Works of the law, 132
Worship, 50
Writings, 58

Zealots, 32
Zechariah, 54, 143
Zedekiah, 98

Index of Scripture References

Genesis

1:3 124
1:6 124
1:24 124
12:3 89
16:10-11 24
18:18 89
22:18 89
25:24 67
26:4 89
28:14 89
35:16-19 22
49:2-28 130

Exodus

2:3 15
3:13-15 126
4:16 134
4:22 21
6:11 124
7:1 135
8:19 10
14:31 114
23:26 67
31:18 10
34:1 130
34:27-28 131

Leviticus

19:2 111
19:18 ...... 54, 133
22:21 67

Numbers

15:3 67
23:19 102

Deuteronomy

4:31 50
6:4-5 133
6:4-9 50
7:6 ...... 111, 132
7:6-11 50
9:10 10
10:12-13 133
13:1-3 ..... 50, 73
17:14-15 108
18:10-12 70
18:15 108
18:15-16 34
18:15-22 50
18:22 72
24:10, 17, 19, 21 . 50
24:16 50
33:10 110

Judges

6:36 70

I Samuel

1:6 130
1:19-20 130
2:6-7 130
5:10 128
9:6 78
9:9 78
10:2 22
14:41-42 69
27:1 124
28:6 70

II Samuel

5:24 70

I Kings

8:41-43 89
11:29-31 76
12:15 76
13:2 78
18:39 128
22:5-23 72

II Kings

9:7 114
14:25-29 84
16:15 70
22:8 49
23:15-17 78
23:22 49
24:6 82
25:29-30 83

I Chronicles

3:17-18 83

Ezra

9:11 114
10:2-4 88

Nehemiah

8:8 55
13:23-31 88

Esther

5:8 67

Job

1:3 129
35:8 102
41:11 95

Psalms

2:7 35
8:4 102
16:10 ...... 34, 35
23:1-3 127
24:1 ff. 95
32:1-2 94
67:2-4 90
72:17 90

74:1-2, 9-10 57
78:2 43
80:17 103
89:39-40 129
110:1 34
118:22-23 63
119:105 137
129:3 129
144:3 102
145:19 67
146:3 103

Proverbs

13:19 67
16:33 69

Isaiah

2:1 138
2:4 91
7:14 23
7:16 75
8:4 75
8:7-8 25
8:10 70
8:16-17 52
8:19 70
9:6-7 99
11:1 27
11:2 99
11:6 100
11:6-9 85
11:9 100
18:1-8 15
19:23-25 89
22:15-19 84
26:19 ...... 48, 92
28:16 95
29:13 42

32:1-2 100
37:33-35 75
38:1-6 76
40:3 27
40:13-14 95
41:8-10 130
41:9 114
42:1-4 20
42:18-25 130
43:10 ..... 114, 130
44:1-5 130
45:14 85
45:22 90
49:6 90
51:12 103
Ch. 53 34
53:12 116
54:11-17 98
55:3 35
56:2 103
56:7 .... 44, 89
60:1 48
61:1-2a 39

Jeremiah

3:16 143
Ch. 7 143
7:11 44
7:14 143
8:11 73
14:13-14 71
18:1-2 124
18:1-3 28
18:7-10 77
20:1-6 84
22:19 82
22:30 83
23:5-6 98

23:9-40 73
26:18 52
27:9-10 71
28:16-17 76
30:1-2 52
31:9 129
31:15 21
31:16-17 22
31:29-30 50
31:31-34 117
32:6-15 28
36:32 52
43:10-13 80

Ezekiel
Ch. 18 50
21:21-22 70
26:7-14 79
29:18-19 79
34:15-16 99
34:24 99
36:25-28 92
37:1-14 92

Daniel
7:12-14 103
7:27 103
12:2-3 92

Hosea
1:2 138
4:12 70
11:1-3 ...... 20, 21

Joel
2:28-29 33
2:32 95
3:2 87
3:13 87
3:19-20 88

Amos
3:7 114
4:6-10 130
7:11 83
9:11-12 99

Micah
1:6 81
3:8 72
3:11 72
3:12 81
4:3 91
5:2 25

Habakkuk
2:14 85

Zephaniah
1:15 87
1:18 87
2:8-15 88

Zechariah
2:11 91
4:6-14 83
6:10-13 83
8:22 91
9:9 28
10:2 71
11:12-13 28
14:16-18 85

Ecclesiasticus
39:1 58
44:1 57
44:21 91
49:15 59

I Maccabees
2:59-60 59

II Maccabees
2:13-14 59
2:59-60 59

Enoch
1:9 47

Matthew
1:12 83
1:22-23 23
2:6 26
2:13-15 20
2:17-18 22
2:23 27
3:1-3 26
3:8-9 145
3:15 67
5:17 40
5:21-22 40
5:23-24 40
5:27-28 40
5:33-37 41
10:40-41 108
11:3-5 101
12:17-21 20
12:38-42 44
13:10-11 41
13:14-16 41
13:34-35 43
16:13-14 107
16:20 101
20:28 105
21:1-7 29
21:11 107
21:12-13 44

Matthew (cont.)
21:43 64
21:46 107
22:35-40 133
23:34-35 48
24:30 105
26:30 63
27:3-10 28
27:43 47
28:19-20 91

Mark
1:2-3 37
1:15 67
2:10-11 105
6:4 108
7:6-7 42
7:13 139
8:27-28 107
8:31 105
9:2-8 120
9:31 105
10:33-34 105
10:45 105
12:24 46
12:26 47
12:28-34 133
13:26-27 105
14:24 113

Luke
2:6 67
2:32 91
3:4 47
4:18-21 39
5:1 139
6:5 104
7:16 107

9:18-19 107
10:25-38 133
11:28 139
11:49-51 48
20:42 47
21:24 67
21:27 105
22:27 105
22:42 106
24:19 107
24:27 14

John
1:1 138
1:14 138
1:17 132
1:29 113
1:51 105
2:22 46
3:13 105
4:19 107
5:47 46
6:14 107
6:27 105
6:32 105
6:53 105
7:40-41 107
9:17 107
10:10 106
14:7 106
17:6 140
18:36 33
20:30-31 18

Acts
1:8 91
2:17-18 33
2:23 34
2:27 34

2:34-35 34
3:18 34
3:22 34
3:22-23 108
4:8, 10-12 65
4:31 138
5:42 96
6:7 138
7:37 108
7:42 47
7:56 105
8:26-40 116
8:32 46
13:15-27 35
13:32-35 35
Ch. 15 30
15:1-29 30

Romans
1:2 46
1:16 31
1:20-32 47
3:25 113
4:7 94
4:16-17 146
5:1 131
5:2 112
5:14-19 105
5:17 147
6:14 131
8:3 113
9:6-7 139
9:25 94
10:11-13 95
11:33-35 95
12:1 148
13:9 66
13:10 67

I Corinthians

1:18 140
2:4-5 140
5:7 113
6:6 148
7:25 142
10:26 95
11:24 118
11:25 118
15:3-4 46
15:3-5 34
15:21-23 105
15:45-50 105

II Corinthians

5:4 47
6:16 147

Galatians

2:16 132
3:9 31
3:10 46
3:24-26 121
3:27-29 146
3:29 31
5:14 67
6:2 149
6:16 145

Ephesians

2:19-22 148
4:15 148
5:14 48
6:11-13 47

Philippians

2:10-11 148

Colossians

1:18 148
1:25-26 139

II Timothy

3:13-17 46
3:15 46

Hebrews

1:1-2 109
1:3 47
3:1 112
3:2-6 148
4:12 140
5:12-14 112
7:1-13 112
8:8-13 118
10:14 118

11:35-36 47
12:28 147
13:15 148

James

1:9 47
2:5 147
2:8 67
4:5 47

I Peter

2:7-8 65
2:17 148
4:17 148

I John

3:10-17 148

Jude

9 47
14-15 47

Revelation

1:13 105
5:12 113
14:14 105
19:10 109